Understanding Jesus Today

WHAT CAN WE KNOW ABOUT JESUS?

Understanding Jesus Today

Edited by Howard Clark Kee

Growing interest in the historical Jesus can be frustrated by diverse and conflicting claims about what he said and did. This series brings together in accessible form the conclusions of an international team of distinguished scholars regarding various important aspects of Jesus' teaching. All of the authors have extensively analyzed the Biblical and contextual evidence about who Jesus was and what he taught, and they summarize their findings here in easily readable and stimulating discussions. Each book includes an appendix of questions for further thought and recommendations for further reading on the topic covered.

Other Books in the Series

What Can We Know about Jesus?

HOWARD CLARK KEE

CAMBRIDGE
UNIVERSITY PRESS

Published by the Press Syndicate of the University of Cambridge
The Pitt Building, Trumpington Street, Cambridge CB2 1RP
40 West 20th Street, New York, NY 10011-4211, USA
10 Stamford Road, Oakleigh, Melbourne 3166, Australia

First published 1990
Reprinted 1991 (twice), 1993, 1995

Printed in the United States of America

Library of Congress Cataloging-in-Publication Data is available.
A catalogue record for this book is available from the British Library.

ISBN 0-521-36057-9 hardback
ISBN 0-521-36915-0 paperback

Contents

Introduction: Knowing Jesus and Knowing about Jesus

Paul was persuaded that he had seen Jesus (1 Cor 9:1). His having seen Jesus was as real to him as was the experience of Jesus reported by the other apostles. This was true even though he had had no association with Jesus during his earthly lifetime such as the disciples had had. Paul's call as an apostle was based on having seen Jesus risen from the dead, as he reports in 1 Corinthians 15:8. There he makes no distinction between his having seen Jesus and the appearances of Jesus to the disciples. Equally important is that apparently they also saw no difference between Paul's experience and theirs, since they accepted him as having been called to apostleship by the risen Christ, just as they had been. But Paul's vision of the living Christ was not his only direct encounter with Jesus. Paul tells in 2 Corinthians 12:9 what the Lord said to him, when once he was taken up into the presence of Christ – who had been exalted to heaven – giving him instruction about enduring the difficulties and sufferings he was undergoing ("My grace is sufficient for you . . ."). It is clear that Paul's claim to know Jesus was based on personal experience. Paul was persuaded that he *knew* Jesus.

This kind of knowledge, which is based on claims of spiritual or mystical encounter, is widely greeted with skepticism in the modern world, as it was by many in ancient times. Yet, in addition to these claims of mystical experience of Jesus, Paul offers in his letters important information as to what he *knows about* Jesus, which has come to him through traditions, handed down by those who preceded him in the early Christian community. As such, it can be critically examined and compared with other testimony from eyewitnesses of Jesus, just as one would evaluate evidence in a modern court or academic setting. For example, when Paul reports the tradition about the Eucharist or communion, he says he received it "from the Lord" (1 Cor 11:23), but the terms he uses for receiving and transmitting show that he is passing on to others in the community what had been passed on to him. The basic details of the eucharistic meal, and even the terminology used – "took," "blessed," "broke," "gave" – match reports from other sources wholly independent of Paul, such as the Gospels (Mk 14:22–4; Mt 26:26–8; Lk 22:17–19). Is Paul's knowledge of Jesus based on firsthand religious experience or on tradition? The answer is, of course, both.

In modern times, Christians commonly claim to have the same ways of "knowing Jesus," based on both personal experience and tradition, but much of the emphasis falls on private encounters with Jesus. For example, there are many hymns and gospel songs in which believers celebrate their associations with Jesus. These range from "In the Garden," with its refrain about Jesus–"He walks with me and he talks with me, and he tells me I am his own" – to the southern spiritual "I Have a Little Talk with Jesus, and I Tell Him All About My Troubles," which ends with the line, "Just a little talk with Jesus makes it right, all right." Yet if all the beliefs of Christians, ancient and modern, about the existence of Jesus were to be based solely on such claims of immediate spiritual experience, skeptics might write off these reports as delusions, falsehoods, or the output of wild imaginations. Yet even those who base their claims of knowing Jesus on private spiritual encounters acknowledge freely that the specifics and the meaning of these experiences are grounded in tradition – that is, on the picture of Jesus that comes through the New Testament, and, especially, through the Gospels.

As early as a century and a half after Jesus was born, there were those in the Roman world – both pagan and Jewish – who sought to discredit Jesus. They suggested that he performed his miracles by means of magic, and scoffed at the notion of his having been born of a virgin. In the Jewish sources, for example, a pun was invented on the Greek word for virgin, *parthenos*, for which was substituted *Pantheros*. Instead of the early Christian claim that Jesus was born of a virgin, the notion was proposed that he was really the illegitimate son of a Roman soldier named Pantheros. What is important for our purposes is that Jesus' detractors sought to destroy his reputation, but did not deny either that he existed or that he performed extraordinary deeds. Similarly, assertions by some modern scholars that Jesus was a magician deny the divine origin of the mission in which Christians have seen him as engaged, but at the same time acknowledge that he did exist and that a major factor in his appeal was his ability to perform healings and other forms of renewal of life.

From the seventeenth century to the present, however, there have been those who have wanted to deny that Jesus ever lived or to discredit completely the Christian reports of his activities. These proposals include the theory that he never truly existed. The skeptics' assumption is that the gospel accounts of Jesus are the product of ancient mythmakers who were seeking to demonstrate his unique relationship to God in fantastic accounts that reached their climax in the fraudulent story of his having been raised from the dead. Other suggestions as to who the "real" Jesus was include (1) that he was really a mildly reforming rabbi whose intentions were misunderstood by the contemporary Jewish leadership and whose followers completely distorted the facts in writing the gospel narratives; and (2) that he began his career as a member of the Essenes, the Jewish monastic sect that lived at Qumran, overlooking the

Dead Sea, while awaiting the end of the age and God's intervention on their behalf. He would establish them in Jerusalem as the true people of God who were to renew and purify the Temple. Jesus, the theory postulates, ran afoul of the political and officially established religious authorities, who conspired to bring about his execution. The question remains as to how we are to bring together the evidence about Jesus from non-Christian sources and relate it to the testimony of the New Testament writers.

In what follows, we shall look in some detail at historical references to Jesus in pagan and Jewish sources from the early centuries after his birth (Chapter 1), in order to see what matches, modifies, supplements, or contradicts reports in the Gospels. In this connection, we shall analyze the probable relationship of Jesus to the various Jewish groups of his day, including the Dead Sea sect. Then we shall turn to the early Christian testimony about Jesus, both that included in the New Testament (apart from the Gospels) and other early Christian writings that claim to offer information about him, including some that have become available only in recent decades (Chapter 2). In Chapters 3 and 4 we shall concentrate on the most important body of evidence for our knowledge of Jesus – that is, on the oldest available forms of access to the gospel evidence. Our primary attention will be first on "Q," the source used by Matthew and Luke that consists primarily of the sayings of Jesus; then we shall analyze the Gospel of Mark, which is the earliest of the Gospels, and which provided the writers of the other three gospels a basic source and structure for their accounts of the public career of Jesus. John, we shall see, follows the Markan pattern in a general way, but offers important differences in detail about Jesus' career and the content of his teaching. It is to an analysis of these other three Gospels – Matthew, Luke, and John – that we turn in the final chapter.

As we examine this range of evidence, we shall see important differences in insight and interpretation, as well as certain common features in the portrayal of Jesus. In a concluding section we shall summarize the results of this inquiry as to "what we can know about Jesus."

Chapter 1

What Can We Learn from Sources Outside the New Testament?

The historical writings dealing with the Roman world in the first century of our era contain very few references to Jesus. This should not be surprising. It was only after the Christian movement had grown in numbers and significance to become an important factor in Roman politics and society that mention of it appeared in the historical sources. Although Acts reports the numbers of converts to Christianity in Jerusalem in the thousands (Acts 2:41; 4:4), the fact that the gatherings of Christians took place in private homes (1 Cor 16:19; Rom 16:23) suggests that participants in the Jesus movement in gentile cities during the first generation probably numbered in the dozens, or scores at the most. The majority of these people were of simple backgrounds, so that their role in society would not have drawn public attention to them. It is precisely those events connected with Jesus and his followers involving encounters with the Roman authorities that appear as the rare allusions to Christianity in sources outside the New Testament.

Evidence from Josephus

The most striking of these references to Jesus appears in the monumental work, *Antiquities of the Jews*, written by the Jewish historian Josephus, who lived from the mid-thirties to the end of the first century A.D. Originally a champion of Jewish national independence, he turned to the role of collaborator with the Romans when they invaded Palestine in A.D. 67–70.

In Josephus' list of Jewish nationalists and troublemakers in the first century he mentions both Jesus and Jesus' brother James, who became the leader of the church in Jerusalem. Unfortunately, the ancient text of Josephus' *Antiquities* that has come down to us gives evidence of having been tampered with by Christians in order to make the Jewish author bear Christian testimony. The relevant text reads as follows:

About this time [i.e., while Pontius Pilate was governor of Judea, A.D. 26–36] there lived Jesus, a wise man, if indeed one ought to call him a man. For he was one who wrought surprising feats and was a teacher of such people as accept the truth gladly. He won over many Jews and many of the Greeks. He was the Messiah. When Pilate, upon hearing him accused by men of the highest standing among us, had condemned him to be crucified, those who had in the first place come to love him did not give up their affection for him. On the third day he appeared to them restored to life, for the prophets of God had prophesied these and countless other marvelous things about him. And the tribe of Christians, so-called after him, has still to this day not disappeared. (*Antiquities* 18.63)

This passage in its present form reads as though Josephus were a Christian – which of course he was not. The distinguished Jewish scholar L. H. Feldman, who made this translation, thinks we should simply omit the sentence, "He was the Messiah." Then we may read the rest of the statement as the author's report of what the Christians claimed about Jesus. If this is a correct evaluation of this section from Josephus, it would reflect his estimate of the movement from the perspective of the late first century, when he was writing this major historical account of Palestinian Judaism. It obviously links the death of Jesus with Pilate as the Gospels do, and specifies that he died by crucifixion. It refers to his unusual abilities, his claim to wisdom, and the fact that both Jews and non-Jews responded to his message. It bears witness to the claim of his followers that God had brought him back from the dead and that in him the promises made to the prophets were fulfilled.

In addition, it notes that his major public role was that of teacher, and that the quality characterizing his relationship to his followers was that of love. Missing is any detailed information as to what he taught or the nature of his remarkable "feats." The remark, "if indeed one ought to call him a man," could be understood to imply that Jesus is divine, but since Josephus gives no hint of having been drawn to Christianity, it more likely originally indicated that Josephus thought Jesus was an agent of Satan. This would fit with the report in the Gospels of an accusation against Jesus by the scribes and Pharisees that he was in league with the prince of demons (Mk 3:22; Mt 9:34). In this extrabiblical evidence there is no denial that Jesus performed extraordinary deeds: The issue is the source of his power.

Evidence from the Roman Historians

Among the letters written by the Roman governor Pliny to the emperor Trajan around the year 110 was one concerning the growth of the Christian movement in Bithynia, a province on the south shore of the Black Sea in what is now Turkey. Earlier, as Pliny told the emperor, the presence of Christians had been evident in the cities of this district, but more recently it had spread to even the rural areas. As a result, there had been an alarming drop in support for and participation in the worship of the gods at the temples promoted officially by the Roman state. More seriously, Pliny continued, the Christians, even under threat of death, refused to offer the appropriate required prayers and gifts to the image of the emperor, who was now officially to be regarded as divine.

When Pliny had investigated what the members of the Christian groups did, he was astounded to find that their behavior was so inoffensive: They gathered early in the morning to sing a hymn to Christ as a god; they took an oath to avoid wicked deeds such as fraud, theft, deceit, or adultery. Pliny was surprised to find that their sacred meal consisted only of ordinary food. Among their leaders were women, who were called deaconesses. The worst he could say about the Christians was that they were subject to a "depraved and excessive superstition." But because they refused to perform the divine honors to the emperor, and therefore threatened the solidarity of local support for his rule, he had offered them the choice of renouncing their faith in Jesus (for which renunciation they could give evidence by their participation in the official ceremonies) or facing execution. Here, as in the evidence from Josephus, several important features of the Jesus movement receive confirmation: the affirmation – in the name of Jesus – of the commandments attributed to Jesus against stealing, false witness, adultery; the importance of the common meal as the central act in which the unity of God's people is confirmed; and the important place of women in the leadership of the church.

In his *Lives of the Twelve Caesars*, Suetonius (A.D. 70–122?) mentions an incident that occurred in Rome during the reign of the emperor Claudius (A.D. 41–54). The Jewish community there had been split apart "at the instigation of Chrestos," he reports. Claudius reacted by driving all the Jews from Rome. It is widely believed that this writer mistook what would have been for him an uncommon title, Christos, for the familiar Greek name Chrestos. What created the disturbance among the Jews in Rome, therefore, was not the arrival of a troublemaking individual with a common name (Chrestos), as Suetonius supposed, but the coming to that group of someone preaching to the Jews about *Christos* – that is, proclaiming Jesus as Messiah. This expulsion of the Jews from Rome by Claudius is also reported in Acts 18:1–4, where we read that two of Paul's original helpers in Corinth, Priscilla and Aquila, had been driven out of Rome along with other Jews. The fact that they were apparently Christians when Paul began his association with them confirms the theory that Jesus was being effectively preached as Messiah to Jews in Rome before the middle of the first century. But otherwise it adds no new information about him.

Another Roman historian, Tacitus (A.D. 55–117?), reports in his *Annals* (15:44) that when the emperor Nero (who ruled from 41 to 54) was suspected of having set Rome on fire, he shifted the blame to the Christians and punished them accordingly. As Tacitus wrote:

Neither human help, nor imperial munificence, nor all the modes of placating heaven, could stifle the scandal or dispel the belief that the fire had taken place by order [i.e., of Nero]. Therefore to scotch the rumor, Nero substituted as culprits and punished with the utmost refinements of cruelty, a class of men, loathed for their vices, whom the crowd style Christians. Christus, the founder of the name, had undergone the death penalty in the reign of Tiberius, by sentence of the procurator Pontius Pilate, and the pernicious superstition was checked for a moment, only to break out once more, not merely in Judea, the home of the disease, but in the capital itself, where all things horrible or shameful in the world collect and find a vogue. First, then, the confessed members of the sect were arrested; next, on their disclosures, vast numbers were convicted, not so much on the count of arson as for their hatred of the human race. And derision accompanied their end: they were covered with wild beasts' skins and torn to death by dogs; or they were fastened on corpses, and when light failed were burned as lamps by night. Nero had offered his gardens for the spectacle, and gave an exhibition in his Circus, mixing with the crowd in the garb of a charioteer, or mounted on his chariot.

Once more, in this excerpt from Tacitus, we have support for the report in the Gospels that Jesus was put to death under Pontius Pilate. The additional information that this took place during the reign of Tiberius (A.D. 14–37) gives us a terminal date for that event (A.D. 37) and, when linked with the term of Pilate's governorship (26–36), points to the year 29 as the most plausible date for Jesus' crucifixion. The vivid account serves also to confirm that three decades later (by the mid-sixties) Christianity had attracted a large number of believers, and that many of them were more willing to renounce their lives than renounce their faith. The detail that they were filled with "hatred of the human race" is probably to be understood as an outsider's interpretation of their concept of Christians as God's elect people, and of their announcement of the coming of the end of the present world order when the Kingdom of God was to be fully established. Here again, we have no new information to supplement what is found in the Gospels, but there is clear confirmation of the historical existence of Jesus, of his death at the hands of the Roman authorities at a specific point in history, and of the launching of the movement that quickly spread to the capital of the empire itself. Within thirty-five years of Jesus' death, the movement he launched was of sufficient size and significance as to provide the emperor of Rome with a scapegoat for his own irresponsible actions in setting fire to the capital.

That the gospel had reached Rome by the middle of the first century, and that it had penetrated even the upper levels of Roman society, may also be confirmed through the writings of Dio Cassius, a later Roman historian (150–235). He reports that Domitilla, a niece of the emperor Domitian (ruled 81–96), was exiled for having lapsed into "Jewish customs" and "atheism" (which means that she had abandoned the worship of the traditional Roman gods and goddesses). This charge against her may point to her having been converted to Christianity, which would have understandably been confused with the similar and familiar religion of Judaism: Both were monotheistic, both appealed to the same sacred scriptures, and both claimed to worship the same God. That inference about Domitilla's conversion to Christianity may be confirmed by the existence in Rome of a catacomb (a string of underground Christian burial chambers) named for her. Thus, by the end of the first century,

Christians may have included among their fellowship even members of the imperial household.

Evidence from the Rabbinic Sources

The evidence from the Jewish sources of the first two or three centuries is more hostile toward Jesus and his movement, although it also confirms his historical existence and the rapid growth of the community that bears his name. Allusions to him in the rabbinic writings are of uncertain date, since the basic documents of rabbinic Judaism were not produced until the period from the second to the sixth centuries. It is impossible to date with certainty those traditions included in this material – known in its final form as the Mishna and the Talmud – which claim that they are quoting rabbis who were (allegedly) active in the first century. Jesus is referred to as "a certain person," on the assumption that even to mention his name would be to give him undue honor. The specific details about this unnamed character and his followers point unmistakably to Jesus. In some passages of this Jewish material, he is called Ben Stada or Ben Pandira or Ben Panthera, implying that he is the illegitimate son (Ben, in Hebrew) of a soldier or some other unworthy person. Similarly, his mother is pictured as disreputable. In a document known as Shabbath (104) the following incident is reported:

Rabbi Eliezer . . . was arrested for Minuth [holding Christian beliefs] and they brought him to the tribunal for judgment. The governor said to him, "Does an old man like you occupy himself with such things?" He said to him, "Faithful is the judge concerning me." The governor supposed that he was saying this of him, but he was not thinking of any but his Father who is in heaven. [The governor] said to him, "Since I am trusted by you, I shall be the same concerning you. . . . Perhaps these societies [the Christians] err concerning these things. *Dismissus*, behold you are released." And when he had been released from the tribunal, he was troubled because he had been arrested for

Minuth. His disciples came to him to console him, but he would not take comfort. Rabbi Aquiba [early second century] came in and said to him, "Perhaps one of the Minim [Christians] has said a word of Minuth and it pleased you." He said, "By heaven, once I was walking in Sepphoris, and I met Jacob of Chepat Sichnin, and he said to me a word of Minuth in the name of Jesus Ben Pantri, and it pleased me. And I was arrested for words of Minuth because I overstepped the words of Torah [the Jewish law]: 'Keep your way far from her, and do not come near the door of her house, because she has cast down many wounded'" [Prv 5:8].

What is significant in this passage is that Jesus' existence and activity as teacher and worker of miracles are simply assumed. It is also apparent that his teaching was on some points so close to that of the Jewish teachers that it was possible for a later rabbi to subscribe to something Jesus had taught, without being fully aware that it stemmed from Jesus and was not merely part of the intra-rabbinic debates. Yet the rebuke to which the unwitting sympathizer was subjected shows that there was something central to the teaching of Jesus that was seen by the rabbinic Jews as a threat to their understanding of right relationship with God. Anyone who held such a view must be called to account by the Jewish authorities. Mention of Sepphoris, an important city in Galilee located only a few miles from Nazareth, shows that Christianity had taken root in Jesus' native territory. If the "governor" is a Roman official, rather than a leader in the Jewish community, the story implies that the Jesus movement was also regarded with suspicion by the political as well as the religious leaders of the land.

Joseph Klausner, a Jewish scholar writing earlier in this century, analyzed the rabbinic traditions about Jesus to determine what those from the earliest strata (the so-called Tannaitic period, which is assumed to be roughly contemporary with the apostles) tell us about him. His conclusions were as follows:

There are reliable statements to the effect that his name was Yeshu'a of Nazareth; that he "practiced sorcery" i.e., performed miracles, as was usual in those days) and beguiled and led Israel astray; that he mocked the words of the wise [the interpreters of the law who came to be regarded as authoritative]; that he expounded the scriptures in the same manner as the Pharisees; that he had five disciples; that he said he was not come to take aught away from the Law or to add to it; that he was hanged [crucified] as a false teacher and beguiler on the eve of the Passover which happened on a Sabbath; that his disciples healed the sick in his name.

The only point of seeming conflict between this Jewish material and the New Testament concerns the number of Jesus' disciples. Although the Gospels and the Acts of the Apostles indicate they were twelve in number, there is also evidence that Jesus had an inner core of followers, as in the story of the Transfiguration (Mk 9:2), where Peter, James, and John alone are invited to accompany him to the mountain. Otherwise the portrait of Jesus conveyed by the rabbinic material matches the gospel evidence well, though it does not supplement it. Later rabbinic tradition intensifies the hostility to Jesus, picturing him as of illegitimate birth, as a sorcerer and deceiver, and, through his revolutionary program, as a fundamental threat to the integrity of the Jewish people. As we shall see, the gospel tradition at some points (especially in the Gospel of Matthew) may actually heighten the hostility between Jesus and his Jewish contemporaries beyond what it was historically.

Another more recent Jewish writer's reconstruction of the relationship of Jesus to Judaism in his time that attracted a wide readership two decades ago is *The Passover Plot* by Hugh Schonfeld. He claimed to base his results on the historical evidence from the New Testament correlated with that from the Jewish documents of the period. It was Schonfeld's theory that for the Jews of that period, "Messiah" meant simply "King of Israel," and that Jesus laid claim to this role. So long as he remained in Galilee, with his core of simple followers, neither the religious nor the Roman political authorities paid much attention to his movement, but when he came to Jerusalem and entered the city as a royal figure (Mk 11, the so-called Palm Sunday entrance into Jerusalem), the religious authorities reported him to the Roman governor as a threat to Judea's political stability.

Schonfeld conjectured that Jesus knew that this triumphal entry would evoke both popular acclaim and official opposition. But he had instructed his followers in advance that he would be put to death, or rather that when he was crucified, they should take him down from the cross when he seemed to have died, and then bury him. When he revived and reappeared, many would be persuaded that he was the Messiah, King of Israel. All went seemingly as Jesus had planned. But when Joseph of Arimathea came to the tomb on the third day (following the Sabbath), although Jesus was still alive, he was so weakened that he died shortly thereafter. Hence his plot to make a public appearance as though he had risen from the dead – which was to have rallied the masses to his cause – never came off. The disciples had seen him alive after his burial, but claimed that, rather than merely dying, he had been taken up to God. The major thrust of the Christian movement is therefore to be seen as a pious fraud, Schonfeld implies. That Jesus actually died on the cross, however, is confirmed by all the evidence available – Jewish, Roman, and Christian. Accordingly, Schonfeld's thesis is sheer conjecture in the face of the evidence, and constitutes uncritical use of the evidence from the Gospels and of assumptions that do not hold up under responsible historical examination. It is not surprising, therefore, that this elaborate theory has passed into the limbo it deserves. But to recall what was once a sensational and widely considered historical hypothesis is to remind ourselves of the care with which the evidence about Jesus – both within and without the New Testament – must be analyzed.

Evidence from the Dead Sea Scrolls

Ever since 1947, when manuscripts dating from the first century A.D. were found in caves overlooking the Dead Sea, there has been speculation that Jesus might have been connected with the group that produced these documents. Archaeologists' discovery of the community center, including the remains of the room where the documents were written and copied, as well as the pools where the group performed baptisms, heightened the interest in the Dead Sea Jewish sect. Of special interest was the uncovering of the remains of the very room where the group gathered for its common meals. An anteroom was discovered, where the dishes were stacked, awaiting the next meal – which did not take place because the Romans destroyed the settlement just before A.D. 70. Also, the remains of a lectern were excavated, from which the Scriptures and perhaps excerpts of the community's own writings apparently were read as the common meal was eaten. From one of the writings it is evident that their main ceremonial meal involved the sharing of bread and wine, in anticipation of the coming of the end of the age. Judging by the size of the meeting room, the group numbered fewer than one hundred residents.

As the documents found there were published in translation, a number of points of similarity between this group and the early Christians fed the speculation about the possibilities of Jesus having been connected with the group. The following similarities between the Dead Sea sect and the early Christians are apparent: Both groups were critical of official Judaism; both practiced baptism, and did so in the Jordan Valley; both ate meals of bread and wine, in expectation of the coming of the Messiah in final triumph; both saw the Scriptures as being fulfilled through their leader; both produced their own writings, which supplemented and reinterpreted the Jewish Bible; both were critical of the official priesthood and the way the worship of God was carried on in the Temple; both awaited the destruction of the Temple. In one of the most recently published of these documents, the Temple Scroll, there is a prediction that the person who violates the integrity of the Covenant people will be put to death by being hanged from a tree (i.e., crucified), and there is counsel to see that he is buried before sundown in order to avoid polluting the holy day.

The result of the comparative study of the Dead Sea Scrolls and the New Testament is to demonstrate beyond doubt that, while the solutions that Jesus offered are significantly different from those of either the Dead Sea community or the subsequent rabbinic movement, the issues he addresses in the gospel tradition are precisely those under debate within Judaism in the period before A.D. 70 – the year the Dead Sea community was destroyed. It shows also how vital the expectation was within first-century Judaism that the present age was coming to an end, to be replaced by the new age in which God would vindicate the faithful and establish his rule over the world. Further, these writings show that the traditional forms of expectation and obligation, based on the Hebrew scriptures, were being radically rethought in this period. It is also evident that the early Christian community – like the Dead Sea sect – regarded ceremonial meals and washings as group expressions of their being prepared for the coming of God's Rule, and that this new age would come through some person or persons chosen and empowered (Anointed = Messiah) by God.

Beyond these similarities, however, the differences between the Jesus tradition and the Dead Sea group are fundamental. The major question for both groups is, who is qualified to share in the new people of God? For the Dead Sea community, there had to be an absolute distinction between their group and everyone else, including all other Jews. They did not consider the other Jews who claimed to be members of the Covenant people as sufficiently strict in obeying the Law, and especially

in observing the rules of ritual purity. The Dead Sea sect believed God was going to rebuild the Temple and place them in
charge. When that happened, all Gentiles, as well as all Jews
who failed to measure up to their standards, would be excluded
from entering. There was to be no Court of the Gentiles, surrounding the central sanctuary as there was in the time of
Jesus, where he spoke of God's House as a place of prayer "for
all nations" (Mk 11:17, quoting Is 56:7).

Jesus' fundamental rejection of the principle of ritual purity
in Mark 7:14–23 is precisely opposed to the standards insisted
on by the Dead Sea group. Instead of the inclusive community
of Jesus, who welcomed and restored the lame, the deaf, the
blind, the poor, and moral and social outcasts, the Dead Sea
community explicitly excluded all such persons as unworthy
of sharing in God's Covenant. The intensification of ritual obligations in the Dead Sea community, such as daily ceremonial
washings, is in direct opposition to Jesus' welcoming into the
fellowship of his followers those who wanted to come, regardless of their ritual, ethical, or ethnic background. Instead of
forcing out of the group those who violated its strict ritual
requirements, as was the case in the Dead Sea community,
Jesus welcomed those who were rejected or despised. In what is
surely one of our most authentic traditions, he characterized
himself as "the friend of tax-collectors and sinners" (Lk 7:34).

The supreme irony for those who want to associate Jesus
with the Dead Sea group lies in the undeniable fact that Jesus
died precisely by the mode of execution that the Dead Sea sect
laid down for anyone who threatened their view of the Covenant: being hanged on a tree until he was dead. If Jesus had a
significant relationship with the Dead Sea community, it was
one of fundamental disagreement and challenge. We may recognize as groundless, therefore, the theory that Jesus and his
followers constituted a secret society based on the principles
and practices found in the Dead Sea Scrolls. Instead of forcing

out of the group those who violated its strict requirements (as was the case in the Dead Sea community), Jesus welcomed those who were rejected and despised on ethnic, ritual, physical, or even moral grounds. Comparing him with the Dead Sea sect sharpens the contrast between his movement and theirs.

The result of the examination of the sources outside the New Testament that bear directly or indirectly on our knowledge of Jesus is to confirm his historical existence, his unusual powers, the devotion of his followers, the continued existence of the movement after his death at the hands of the Roman governor in Jerusalem, and the penetration of Christianity into the upper strata of society in Rome itself by the later first century. Sources outside the Gospels show us also that the issues that were Jesus' major concerns in the gospel tradition were precisely those being debated within Judaism of his day – especially the question of qualification for participation in the Covenant people. Before analyzing what the gospel tradition reports about these aspects of Jesus' teachings and public activity, we turn now to what we can learn about him from the early Christian writings apart from the Gospels.

Chapter 2

What Can We Learn from Early Christian Writings Outside the Gospels?

Having examined the non-Christian sources for knowledge of Jesus, are there resources other than the Gospels to which we can turn in our search? Because, as we shall see, the Gospels were written beginning in the last third of the first century, we may ask if there are earlier Christian writings that provide us information about the historical figure of Jesus. Or are there materials produced after the Gospels were written that give access to important information that supplements or corrects what the Gospels convey?

Our quest for Christian sources that predate the Gospels leads us first to Paul, since his letters are the oldest documents preserved in the New Testament and therefore are our most ancient Christian sources. In addition to information from the letters of Paul, we shall also briefly consider similar traditions about Jesus from other early Christian literature, both within and outside the New Testament, before we turn in Chapters 3 and 4 to an analysis of the Gospels and their sources. Careful scrutiny of the nongospel evidence shows that there is an important confirmation of details, even though some of the major features of the gospel tradition about Jesus are only rarely mentioned or are given no place at all in these other writings. Accordingly, traditions about Jesus from Christian sources within and outside the New Testament that provide supplemental information must be evaluated on their own merits.

Our procedure in surveying this evidence will be to move from theme to theme concerning Jesus, looking first at what

Paul wrote on each, and then at what appears in other New Testament writings. Finally, we shall examine briefly a range of early Christian writings to see what they tell us about Jesus. These sources include (1) leading thinkers in the church of the second and third centuries; and (2) the so-called apocryphal "gospels" and "acts" that claim to expand or codify what we can learn from the New Testament about Jesus and his followers. These writings include some manuscripts found only recently in Egypt and Jordan.

Themes from the Gospels in Other
New Testament Writings

Jesus' Human Origin

There is in all these writings the affirmation or the assumption of the historical existence of Jesus. Paul is explicit in his references to Jesus' human descent (Rom 1:4) and birth (Gal 4:4). He mentions that earlier (prior to his conversion) he had regarded Jesus from a purely human point of view (2 Cor 5:16). Even though he affirms the preexistence of Jesus in the presence of God, he depicts him as assuming human form (Phil 2:6). This same point of Jesus' historicity is made in New Testament writings as different as Acts 1:1–2, where his earthly, human activities are referred to, and Hebrews 2:14, where Jesus' partaking of human nature is affirmed. 1 John 1:1–3 and 4:2 assert explicitly that Jesus' followers experienced him in human form through sight, hearing, and touch.

The Historical Event of Jesus' Death

Even more frequently, the New Testament writers speak of his death, and of its significance for God's people. Obviously, death is conceivable only for those who, in common human terms, have lived historical existences. Paul always links his references to Jesus' death with claims of the significance of that event for human reconciliation with God. A selection of Pauline texts where this point is made should include Galatians 1:3; Romans 5:6–18 and 8:3; 1 Corinthians 1:30; and 2 Corinthians 5:18. In 1 Corinthians 15:3, the added point is made that this understanding of Jesus' death is not something Paul thought up, but is part of the tradition that was transmitted to him.

Paul describes the death of Jesus as his having given himself "for our sins" (Gal 1:3) or having humbled himself "unto death, even death on the cross" (Phil 2:8). Thus his death is a real human event (1 Thes 4:10), carried out by human agents (1 Thes 2:15). It is not merely that he gave the appearance of having died, as is the case with certain divine or mythological figures in the ancient world. For example, Osiris, the Egyptian fertility god (who represented the annual cycle of flooding and slackened flow of the Nile), was said to die and be raised from the dead each year. But this was primarily a symbol of the yearly agricultural pattern of the Nile Valley, in which the river during part of the year fertilized the fields along its banks, and then receded in the dry season. In Hebrews 7:26–7, where he is portrayed in the dual role of priest and sacrificial victim, Jesus is described as offering himself up "once for all." The same theme is elaborated in Hebrews 9:11–28. And in Hebrews 13:12 there is mention of the specific detail of Jesus' having been taken outside Jerusalem to be put to death, as the Gospels report. 1 Peter 2:21–4 gives details of his attitude toward his persecutors, including his refusal to respond with bitterness toward those who are about to put him to death. The initiative in sacrificing himself for others is his, and he is portrayed as a most sensitive, compassionate human being. In all these passages, Jesus is pictured as a historical person whose complete humanity is evident in his suffering and death.

The Encounters with the Risen Jesus

As we have noted, the Resurrection is attested by Paul on the basis of his personal experience of meeting the risen Jesus (1 Cor 15:5–9). For Paul, it is as much a fact of past history (Rom 1:5) as is the death of the obedient, suffering, crucified Jesus (Phil 2:9). He declares that those who saw the risen Jesus numbered "more than five hundred" (1 Cor 15:6), in addition to the apostles and including himself (1 Cor 15:7–8). He notes that many of those who saw the risen Jesus are still alive, implying that skeptics can confirm the testimony of Paul and others through one of these many living witnesses. The same mode of understanding Jesus' death and resurrection as historical events is evident in such later New Testament writings as Colossians 2:12 and 1 Peter 3:18.

Although it obviously cannot be considered a historical event – something that happened in the past – Paul and the other New Testament writers share a conviction about Jesus that, from the modern rationalist perspective, is even more incredible than their common belief in the Resurrection on the same historical level with Jesus' death: his coming to earth again. The Resurrection is seen by them as a past event that serves as a prelude to Jesus' return in triumph over the powers of evil (1 Cor 15:23). On that day, all Christians will be called to account for their faithfulness – or lack of it – in the responsibilities that have been placed upon them by God (Phil 1:6, 10; 2 Cor 5:10; 1 Thes 4:17; 5:23). Much of 2 Thessalonians (especially 1:7–12 and 2:8) is taken up with the description of this event at the conclusion of the present age, which for Paul is as historically certain as are the events of Jesus' past. And the event of Jesus' coming and bringing under judgment all the human race is a central theme in the Book of Revelation. Quite apart from the trustworthiness of these predictions about the future, these features – as we shall note in our analysis of the gospel tradition – correspond closely with the message of Jesus as it is conveyed in the Gospels. Thus the New Testament writers' confidence about the future rests on past events that they are convinced have occurred – in many cases, within their own personal experience.

The Teachings of Jesus

The ties between Paul's expectation of Jesus' return and Jesus' announcements of his role in the future coming of God's Rule on earth raise the larger question of the correspondence between the sayings and actions of Jesus reported in the Gospels and the evidence from other New Testament writings. Here again, although the similarities are few, they are striking and serve as significant historical links to Jesus. For example, only two of Jesus' ethical commands in the gospel tradition also appear in the letters of Paul: the command to love, and the instruction about divorce and remarriage (Mk 10:1–12; 12:28–34). The basic requirement to love one's neighbor is affirmed by Paul twice in Romans (Rom 13:9–10; 15:1–3), and in 1 Thessalonians 4:2. In Galatians 6:2 the love command is specifically identified as "the law of Christ."

When Paul decreed to the Corinthians that a woman should not separate from her husband, he specified that it was "not I but the Lord" – meaning Jesus – who gave such a command. The same passage from Genesis 2:24 that is quoted by Jesus in Mark 10:7 appears in Ephesians 5:31–3 as an appeal for mutual love between husbands and wives in the Christian community.

A unique report of a saying of Jesus appears in Acts 20:35, where Paul is reported to have told the delegation of church leaders from Ephesus to remember "the words of the Lord Jesus, how he said, 'It is more blessed to give than to receive.'" This saying is not found in any other source, within or outside the New Testament, but the attribution of this saying to Jesus shows how important the tradition of his teachings was for moral instruction within the early Christian communities.

Events in the Career of Jesus

Two events in the life of Jesus as reported in the Gospels are also mentioned in the other New Testament writings. One of these, the Transfiguration, is referred to only once: in 2 Peter 1:17–18. Significantly, the writer of this letter wants to lend authority to what he is communicating by describing himself as one who was present when this event took place.

The event for which there are multiple references outside the Gospels, however, is the Eucharist or Last Supper. We shall see in our later analyses of the Gospels the variety of details through which this central event is depicted in the gospel tradition. But it is noteworthy that Paul not only refers to the final meal of Jesus (including the quotation of the words he spoke on that occasion), but he also claims that the tradition was given to him by "the Lord." He is merely passing on to the church at Corinth what he received from Jesus – presumably through the Jesus tradition as transmitted in the very first Christian communities' narratives of this event.

It is worth noting in passing that in the later Pauline tradition there is the continuing assumption that the ethical rules that are to guide the Christian communities are based on "the sound words of our Lord Jesus Christ" (1 Tm 6:3). The moral appeal in these later writings builds on the tradition that Jesus is one who called his followers to obedience.

Jesus and the Working of Miracles

Although neither Paul nor the other New Testament writers – with the notable exception of the author of Acts – describes any of Jesus' miracles or those of any of his followers, Paul does refer to healings, signs, and wonders as evidence of the Spirit's work among his people. In 1 Corinthians 12:9, healing is one of the gifts of the Spirit, and healers are listed among the roles of leadership in the churches (1 Cor 12:28). Indeed, the ability to perform signs and wonders is one of the signs of an apostle (2 Cor 12:12). We shall consider in a moment how healings, signs, and wonders comparable to those of Jesus in the gospel tradition are reported as performed by the apostles in Acts. But first it is essential to note that healings and miracles were perceived from the beginning of the Christian movement as indications of continuity between what Jesus had done and what his followers were now enabled to accomplish.

Throughout Acts the writer depicts the apostles as performing the same kind of miracles as are attributed to Jesus in the Gospel of Luke, which is the first of two volumes: Luke–Acts. Peter heals a lame man (Acts 3:6). Philip performs an exorcism (8:5–8). Ananias restores Paul's sight, after he was blinded at the time of his conversion (9:17). Peter heals the paralyzed Aeneas (9:34), and Paul heals a lame man (9:14). In Acts 20 Paul restores a man to life. The claim is made explicit that the capacity to heal is granted by God and becomes effective through the name of Jesus (4:27–31). So powerful is this name that some professional exorcists try to exploit it for their own purposes (19:13–14). Thus the picture is consistent: Jesus is known to the readers of Acts, and presumably to those who have heard of him, as one by and through whom miraculous deeds have been and continue to be performed. His historical existence as a wonder-worker is simply assumed by members and nonmembers of the Jesus movement.

Jesus' Predictions of Divine Judgment on the Jewish Covenant People

Two other aspects of the Jesus tradition are evident in the rest of the New Testament as well: the prediction of the destruction of the Temple as the place where God dwells among his people; and the redefinition of the Covenant people. On the first issue, Paul makes repeated reference to the fact that the new Temple of God is his people, the church. Using the metaphors of architectural construction, Paul describes the new edifice that God is erecting, the foundation of which is Jesus Christ (1 Cor 3:10–17). But he goes on to say that the believers are themselves God's temple, and that God's Spirit dwells among them. He affirms that directly in 2 Corinthians 6:16: "We are the temple of the living God." Imagery making the same basic point is to be found in 1 Corinthians 6:19 and Romans 12:1. This figure is elaborated in Ephesians 2:14–20, where the "household of God" is said to be growing into "a holy temple in the Lord." Similarly, 1 Peter 2:5 depicts the community of the faithful as built into a spiritual house and serving as a royal priesthood. As we shall see, this matches well with the implications of Jesus' prediction of the destruction of the Temple – an utterance that may well have served historically as the final force that united the political and religious leadership in the attempt to be rid of him.

Such a claim made by Jesus, or in his name, would have constituted a threat to his Jewish contemporaries. Perhaps even more threatening would have been the claim, for which there is abundant evidence from Paul and elsewhere in the New Testament, that he redefined both membership and standing within the Covenant people. Paul's own approach to redefining the Covenant people is directly linked with Jesus Christ. In the community of his followers, as Paul asserts in what may be his oldest preserved letter (Gal 3:25–6; 4:5), all the distinctions that have been operative in Jewish self-definition are done away with. These include Jew/gentile, male/female, slave/free. Neither circumcision nor the dietary regulations that had been the historic features of Jewish identity are in effect in the new people of God. Paul sees those liberated from these requirements as the true children of Abraham (Gal 3:29–4:7). In

Romans 9–11 he is still struggling with what this radical inno-
vation implies for the destiny of historic Israel, but he does not
make any concessions about laying down legal requirements
for covenantal participation. All who trust in Jesus are children
of God.

Activities of Jesus beyond the Earthly Realm

There is one interesting incident said to have occurred during
the career of Jesus that is not reported in the Gospels, but
which is described briefly in one of the later New Testament
writings. 1 Peter 3:19 mentions Jesus' having "preached to the
spirits in prison." This is apparently a reference to the opportunity Jesus is said to have been provided by God to preach the
message of human redemption to those who lived before the
Flood and who had failed to respond in faith and obedience to
what God had told them. "In prison" seems to mean that there
was a place where the spirits of the dead were kept in a kind of
storage (underground?) awaiting final decisions about their
eternal fate. That corresponds to ideas that appear in both Judaism and Greek mythology from the time of Jesus, and which
apparently found their way into some early Christian thinking.
It is an idea that survives in some forms of the Christian creeds
that declare that Jesus, after his crucifixion and burial, "de-
scended into hell," the abode of the spirits of the dead. There is
no documentation for this elsewhere in the New Testament,
and certainly no hint of it in the Gospels. The appearance of
this odd detail in a New Testament writing should prepare us
for other strange supplements to New Testament accounts of
Jesus' words and works.

Evidence from the Apocryphal Gospels and Acts

The traditions about Jesus that appear in documents from the
second and subsequent centuries are found in writings that in

some ways resemble the canonical Gospels, as well as in collections of the sayings of Jesus. Of special interest are those documents concerned with what Jesus is reported to have said, as distinct from what he is said to have done. Other writings from the second and subsequent centuries claim to report his activities as well. The sources for this extrabiblical evidence about Jesus can be classified under four headings: (1) forms that resemble the canonical Gospels; (2) Jewish-Christian gospels; (3) Gnostic or secret gospels; and (4) writings that supplement the narratives in the Gospels. The question of whether these sources provide additional reliable information about Jesus must be considered. Our procedure will be to evaluate the evidence as we summarize it.

Canonical-like Gospels

The material that most closely resembles what we find in the canonical Gospels appears in collections of sayings of Jesus. Some of these sayings are merely variants of what we find in the familiar Gospels, usually introduced by the simple formula, "Jesus says . . . ." Ancient copies of these traditions were found in the latter part of the nineteenth century and in the present century in Egypt; they were written on papyrus, which survives remarkably well in arid regions. One fragment, for example, reproduces – with the transposition of a single word – part of Luke 6:42: "And then you can see clearly to pull out the mote that is in the eye of your brother" (*Pap. Oxy.* 1.1). Others are expansions or modifications of the canonical sayings, as in *Papyrus Oxyrhynchus* 1.31–6, which reworks Luke 4:23–4: "Jesus says: A prophet is not acceptable in his own country, neither does a physician work cures on those who know him." This is a reworking of Luke 4:24, where only the unacceptability of the prophet is mentioned. The isolated saying could be a more original form, which Luke condensed, or – as seems more likely – it could be a development of a parallel saying derived from Luke 4:23, where the physician is mentioned.

Other sayings from these sources not only have no parallels in the canonical Gospels, but also stand in tension with what the latter attribute to Jesus. In contrast to the repeated charges that Jesus violated the Sabbath and failed to observe the rules about fasting, *Papyrus Oxyrhynchus* 1.4–11 reads, "Jesus says: If you do not fast to the world, you will not find the kingdom of God, and if you do not keep the Sabbath as Sabbath, you will not see the Father." Or again, in Luke 7:34, Jesus quotes his detractors as saying about him, "Behold a glutton and a drunkard, a friend of tax-collectors and sinners." But *Papyrus Oxyrhynchus* 1.11–22 reports: "Jesus says: I stood up in the midst of the world, and in the flesh I appeared to them and found all drunken, and none found I athirst among them, and my soul is troubled for the sons of men, because they are blind in their heart." Clearly we are faced with incompatible claims: Either Jesus was an ascetic and a strict observer of the Jewish laws about Sabbath and fasting, as this later sayings tradition indicates, or he was a free, life-enjoying person, cordial toward those excluded from the religious community by Jewish law and custom, as the canonical Gospels portray him. Yet even the later sayings tradition does not uniformly picture Jesus as a law-abiding ascetic: Another papyrus fragment, *Papyrus Oxyrhynchus* 10.175, records a tradition that is closer to that of the canonical Gospels (Mk 2:16–17) on precisely the point of Jesus' open attitude toward the excluded: "And the scribes and Pharisees and priests, when they saw him, were angry that with sinners he reclined at table. But Jesus heard it and said: The healthy need not the physician."

The tradition that most closely resembles what we find in the canonical Gospels, therefore, does not provide significant additional information about Jesus. It consists almost entirely of sayings and thus adds no new narrative detail. Or it merely

paraphrases what the four canonical Gospels report Jesus to
have said. Or it stands in such sharp contradiction to what the
canonical Gospels show us to have been the ground of his
conflict with the Jewish leadership that the Gospels of the
New Testament have to be given preference over the later tradition as historically more reliable.

Jewish–Christian Gospels

Mention of the Jewish leadership recalls the second possible
source of information about Jesus from outside the New Testament: the so-called Jewish–Christian gospels referred to by
various writers in the early church. Chief among these is the
Gospel according to the Hebrews. Often mentioned by writers
from the second to the fourth century, no copy has ever been
found, and no extensive quotations have survived in the writings of others. Origen of Alexandria (early third century) quotes
from this gospel a saying of Jesus' about his having been carried
by his mother, the Holy Spirit, who took him by one of his
hairs and transferred him to Mount Tabor. Origen obviously thinks little of the document. And Eusebius, the fourth-
century church historian, regards it as a writing used by some
who have perverted the message of Jesus.

The boldest claim made on behalf of the Gospel of the
Hebrews is by Jerome, who asserts that he personally translated it from Hebrew into Greek and Latin, and that the original was written by Matthew. Later he qualified his statement
about Matthew's authorship, saying only that some make this
claim. But Jerome's line of argument that the original Gospel of
Matthew must have been written in Hebrew because the
quotations are from the Hebrew original, rather than from the
Old Greek Bible (Septuagint), is simply false. The Gospel of
Matthew is in fact based on the Gospel of Mark, in which the
biblical quotations are from the Greek, and not from a Hebrew

original. It appears that Jerome and others in the early church were attracted by the notion of a Hebrew original for the gospel tradition, on the assumption that such a source would take one back to Jesus more directly than would a Greek gospel. But all the evidence shows this to be wishful thinking: The oldest evidence available is in Greek. It should be noted, however, that Greek was the common language of the Mediterranean world in this period, and that at the time of the birth of Jesus so few Jews spoke Hebrew or Aramaic (which had become the major Semitic language of the Middle East) that the Bible had to be translated into Greek if most Jews were to understand it. Only when the rabbinic movement became the dominant option for Jews, following the destruction of the Temple and the defeat of the Jewish nationalists in the early second century, were Hebrew and Aramaic restored as the major religious languages for Jews.

Gnostic Gospels

Considerable interest, both scholarly and popular, was evoked by the discovery in upper Egypt in 1945 of a library of documents from a Gnostic settlement at a place known as Nag Hammadi. When the contents of the library were translated and published in 1977, interest focused particularly on the Gospel of Thomas. Quotations from this writing were known from the writers in the second and subsequent centuries of the church, and from the collections of sayings of Jesus found in the papyrus fragments from Egypt. The writings found at Nag Hammadi were in Coptic, a form of Egyptian written mostly in Greek characters that is used to the present day by Egyptian Christians.

The Gospel of Thomas has no narrative, but consists entirely of sayings of Jesus, prefaced by the note, "These are the secret words which the living Jesus spoke, and Didymus Judas Thom-

as wrote them down." Many of the sayings have no parallels in
the canonical Gospels. For example, "Jesus said: Blessed is the
lion which the man shall eat, and the lion become man; and
cursed is the man whom the lion shall eat, and the lion become
man" (Gosp. Thos. 7). A theme that recurs throughout the document is the secret, timeless knowledge that has been provided
to the chosen ones. For example, "Jesus said: Blessed are the
solitary and the elect, for you shall find the kingdom; for you
came forth thence, and you shall go there again" |Gosp. Thos.
49]. "Jesus said: If they say to you, Whence have you come?,
tell them: We have come from the light, the place where the
light came into being through itself alone. It (stood), and it
revealed itself in their image. If they say to you: Who are you?,
say: We are his sons, and we are the elect of the living Father. If
they ask you: What is the sign of your Father in you?, tell them:
It is a movement and a rest" |Gosp. Thos. 50). Variants of sever-
al of the well-known parables of Jesus appear in the Gospel of
Thomas, sometimes in shorter, sometimes in longer versions.

Perhaps the most revealing of the sayings in the Gospel of
Thomas is the elaborate variant on Jesus' statement in Mark
10:13–16 (Mt 19:13–15; Lk 18:15–18) about entering the kingdom of God as a child. In the familiar gospel contexts, the point
seems to be that children are open and eager to receive what is
offered to them, rather than worrying about their worthiness.
But in the Gospel of Thomas, the child is the representative of
asexuality, on the assumption that in the biblical tradition God
created male and female by dividing Adam. The text in Thomas reads:

Jesus saw some infants at the breast. He said to his disciples: These
little ones at the breast are like those who enter into the kingdom.
They said to him: If we then be children, shall we enter the kingdom?
Jesus said to them: When you make the two one, and when you make
the inside as the outside, and the outside as the inside, and the upper
as the lower; and when you make the male and the female into a

single one, that the male be not male and the female female; when you make eyes in the place of an eye, and a hand in place of a hand, and a foot in place of a foot, an image in place of an image, then you shall enter (the kingdom). (22)

As in the case of the sayings that imply that Jesus was an ascetic, one must choose between two incompatible ways of picturing him: as one who affirms the basic and enduring goodness of human sexuality evident in God's having created human beings as male and female (Mk 10:6; cf. Gn 2:4); or as embodying the hope of being freed from sexual identity expressed in the text just quoted from the Gospel of Thomas. The tradition about becoming as a child and the saying about human sexuality as being inherent in God's creation of humanity are in direct sequence in Mark 10. What seems evident is that the Gospel of Thomas represents a reworking of the Jesus tradition in the second century by Gnostics. This group regarded the natural world as the work of an alien power rather than of God. According to them, Jesus, as a redeemer figure, came from the realm of the true God to disclose the truth to receptive human beings. He became temporarily (or merely appeared to become) involved in the physical universe, but subsequently escaped from it. His major aim, according to this Gnostic group, was to enable those who received the knowledge that he imparted (that is what "Gnostic" means) to escape from the physical universe to the realm of light with him. For some of the Gnostics, superiority to the physical world of creation was to be demonstrated by libertine behavior, while for other Gnostics, a strict ascetic life-style displayed their superiority to the physical universe. All the features of the Gospel of Thomas that we have noted fit this scheme: the ascetic rules, the coming of knowledge from beyond this world, the setting aside of physical existence in its sexual mode. In short, the Gospel of Thomas does not provide earlier tradition about Jesus, but gives evidence of one of the ways in which the tradition was being adapted in the second and subsequent centuries. Additional evidence of this modification of the gospel tradition may be seen in such documents as Sophia Jesu Christ (Wisdom of Jesus Christ) and the Apocryphon of John. In all these late writings, Jesus is a conveyor of secret wisdom. None of the basic functions that he fulfills in the older gospel tradition – as healer, exorcist, and above all, as the one who dies on the cross – is assigned to him in these late, esoteric, speculative writings.

A Secret Gospel?

One document referred to by the late-second-century writer Clement of Alexandria (d. 215) is the Secret Gospel of Mark. In his sharp criticism of a Gnostic group, known as the Carpocratians, Clement charges them with having made public and seriously corrupted the Secret Gospel. Its original form was a collection of secret information about Jesus' words and acts that Mark had obtained in Rome from Peter. This material was to be reserved for the initiated members of the church, and an abbreviated and edited version was to be available for those seeking admission. The latter was the Gospel of Mark as it appears in the New Testament. The Secret Gospel was taken to Alexandria by Mark, Clement reported, and was kept secret there, until the Carpocratians enticed someone in the church to make a copy. When they distributed the secret version, they modified it to support their scandalously libertine life-style.

In 1973, Morton Smith, a historian at Columbia University, claimed that in 1958 he had found a copy of a letter from Clement concerning this secret gospel. He said he had discovered it as part of the binding of a book in the library of Mar Saba Monastery in Palestine, east of Jerusalem. Smith's report echoes that of John of Damascus (715–50), a scholar in the Eastern church, who wrote that he had found a collection of letters of Clement of Alexandria at Mar Saba. The library there, however, was destroyed by fire in the eighteenth century, although damaged manuscripts and ancient volumes may have survived the disaster. What Smith claims to have found is a late-eighteenth-century copy of a letter from Clement to one Theodore (identity unknown). In the letter, Clement distinguishes our Gospel of Mark from the secret version, which was a more spiritual gospel, intended to lead those initiated in the Christian mysteries into the innermost sanctuary of truth. Smith thinks that the "mystery of the kingdom of God" (cf. Mk 4:11) was a baptism administered by Jesus to chosen disciples at night and in the nude (cf. Mk 14:51–2), and that it included physical union. This would represent the licentious segment of the Gnostic movement, so that such a portrait of Jesus as one who practiced homosexual acts would fit well with the libertine behavior of the Gnostic group that Clement claimed had not only published the Secret Gospel of Mark, but had also perverted it. Some scholars, while not sharing Smith's theory about the nature of the mystery, have accepted the idea that there was a Secret Gospel of Mark, of which our canonical Mark is an abbreviated version. In this recently discovered letter – some critics suggest that it is a modern forgery – two narratives appear that are not found in Mark: the story of Jesus' raising a young man from the dead, and an account of the disapproval of Jesus by the boy's mother and a friend of hers. The implication of the latter tale is that they resented the homosexual relations Jesus was having with his male associates.

What seems a far more plausible explanation for this material is that the main group of Christians in second-century Alexandria was both attracted and repelled by the teachings of the Gnostics. While rejecting their libertine life-style, Clement and his fellow Christians built up the notion of secret knowledge as given by God through Jesus to his followers. In the canonical Mark, and in other parts of the gospel tradition, the "mystery of the Kingdom of God" clearly refers to the new age that is about to come, in which the powers of evil will be overcome and God's rule will triumph. Jesus is pictured as giving his disciples clues as to how this will occur, as well as a share in making it happen, through the message they preach and the acts of healing and exorcisms they perform. But as that expectation faded in the second century, and as the Christian leadership was more powerfully influenced by philosophical speculation, there was an inevitable tendency to stress the private information that Jesus is said to have brought to his own. Until the letter is studied by those who do not share Smith's interpretation of it, no one can be sure of its antiquity or its authenticity. But as is the case with the other non-New Testament material that we have surveyed, it stands in sharp contrast to the picture of Jesus that comes through the canonical texts and that is reflected in the secular references to Jesus from the first and second centuries. Equally important is that the values and concerns expressed in this material fit well with what we know from other sources of the church and Roman society in the late second, third, and fourth centuries, even though they are largely incompatible with the New Testament itself.

Supplemental Gospels

Finally we may look briefly at another kind of document that claims to supplement what we learn about Jesus through the canonical Gospels. These are apocryphal gospels that offer details about the events connected with Jesus' birth and death. In the Infancy Gospel of Thomas, for example, we read about Jesus' behavior as a child. Two examples will make clear the aims and values in this material:

(2.1) When this boy Jesus was five years old he was playing at the ford of a brook, and he gathered into pools the water that flowed and made it clean at once, and commanded it by his word alone. He made soft clay and fashioned from it twelve sparrows. And it was the sabbath when he did this. And there were also many other children playing with him. Now when a certain Jew saw what Jesus was doing in his play on the sabbath, he at once went and told Joseph his father; "See, your child is at the brook, and he has taken clay and fashioned twelve birds and has profaned the sabbath." And when Joseph came to the place and saw it, he cried out to him, saying: "Why do you do on the sabbath what ought not to be done?" But Jesus clapped his hands and cried to the sparrows: "Off with you!" And the sparrows took flight and went away chirping. The Jews were amazed when they saw this, and went away and told their elders what they had seen Jesus do.

A vindictive streak in Jesus is portrayed in another part of the Infancy Gospel of Thomas:

(3.1) But the son of Annas the scribe was standing there with Joseph; and he took a branch of a willow and with it dispersed the water which Jesus had gathered together. When Jesus saw what he had done he was enraged and said to him: "You insolent, godless dunderhead, what harm did the pools and the water do to you? See, now you also shall wither like a tree and shall bear neither leaves nor root nor fruit." And immediately that lad withered up completely; and Jesus departed and went into Joseph's house. But the parents of him that was withered took him away, bewailing his youth, and brought him to Joseph and reproached him: "What a child you have, who does such things!"

The Protevangelium of James and the Acts of Pilate offer similar miracle-laden details concerning the events prior to the birth of Jesus, those connected with his trial and execution, and those describing his descent into hell. Apart from stimulating pious curiosity and imagination, these writings add nothing to our historical knowledge of Jesus. Their implicit claim is that they supplement our knowledge of Jesus, but in fact they present a significantly different picture of him than is compatible with the earlier sources. Thus the sayings-type gospels imply a Jesus whose major interest was to enlighten the inner circle of his followers, rather than to preach good news to the alienated and the outcast, as the New Testament represents him. The later narrative gospels present Jesus as partly showing off and partly retaliatory – neither of which characteristics is compatible with the way he is depicted in the canonical Gospels or even in the non-Christian historical references to him. In our search for knowledge about Jesus, we are led, therefore, to the primary sources: the Gospels of our New Testament.

Chapter 3

What Can We Learn from the Oldest Gospel Source?

Christians born in the later decades of the first century were eager to hear directly from the disciples of Jesus what he had said and done. That eagerness is perhaps best expressed by Papias, who was born about A.D. 70 and was bishop of Phrygia in Asia Minor until his death in about 155. Only fragments of his extensive writings have survived (in Eusebius' *Church History* III.39). In them Papias describes how he sought to learn from those who had been associated with Jesus' disciples, such as Andrew or Peter, or from any other apostles, concerning Jesus' acts. He comments, "For I imagined that what was to be obtained from books was not so profitable to me as what came from the living and abiding voice."

Two important factors are evident here: (1) The process of transmitting orally the reports of what Jesus said and did went on even after there were written records, such as the Gospels; and (2) there were those who preferred the oral to the written records. These attitudes are very different from those in our time, in which people in search of what they consider to be truth rather than gossip scorn oral reports as "mere hearsay," preferring instead documentary accounts of what happened in the past. It is not surprising, therefore, that there would have existed sources that predate and underlie the Gospels, which display the freedom and fluidity we might expect in an oral source. Such sources almost certainly existed simultaneously with – and even prior to – our earliest written gospel, Mark.

What Is Q?

One such source – the existence and contents of which can be inferred from two of our Gospels – is one that seems to have been used by Matthew and Luke. Each of these writers seems to have drawn on this source, and to have modified it slightly in order to serve his particular aims. Known by scholars as Q (from the German word for source, *Quelle*), it consists mostly of the sayings of Jesus, although it refers at crucial points to his activities as well. The contents of Q can be determined with reasonable certainty by a careful comparative study of Matthew and Luke at those points where they are presenting the same material, but offering tradition that is not found in Mark, who did not use Q. At many points, of course, Matthew and Luke diverge widely from each other, and one can only assume that where they present unique material they are drawing on independent sources, organizing the material as a whole to suit their own individual purposes. But where they agree and are not dependent on Mark, it looks as though Q is a source they both utilized. And from this material common to Matthew and Luke, Q can be reconstructed.

Careful analysis of the Q material shows that in it Jesus is assumed to be a prophet who was commissioned and empowered by God to announce the end of the present age, and who was warning his followers that he and they must be prepared for suffering before the new age arrives. Some of these predictions are attributed to "the wisdom of God" (for example, Lk 11:49–51). But the content of the message of wisdom shows us that Q is not concerned with proverbial or timeless wisdom. Instead, this source pictures Jesus as having been given special insight and information about what God intends to do and what this plan implies for his faithful people. Throughout the Q material, the followers of Jesus are directly addressed with warnings, instructions, promises, and insights concerning what God is in the process of doing through Jesus.

Because Q as we have it is not a document but a body of material whose contents can only be inferred from other writings, no one can be certain of its precise wording. It seems likely, however, that on the whole Luke has done less editing of the Q material than Matthew has. This conclusion is based on the fact that many words and phrases that appear in Matthew's use of his Markan source, as well as in material that is found only in Matthew, are also found in Matthew's version of the Q material. Examples of this are his repeated references to "righteousness," and his use of the term "kingdom of heaven" instead of "Kingdom of God." Although Luke also uses multiple sources and omits portions of Mark, arranging the whole to serve his overall purposes (see Chapter 5, Luke and the Inclusive Message of Jesus), the fact that he seems not to have adapted the Q material (as Matthew has obviously done) helps to confirm the widely held scholarly view that Luke's version of Q is closer to the original. Matthew, on the other hand, has adapted Q as well as Mark in order to serve his own distinctive ends. Accordingly, we shall follow Luke's version of the Q material in our analysis of it, and all our references to Q are taken from Luke. Our procedure will be to examine Q by themes, rather than merely taking the material in the order in which it appears in the Gospels as we have them. Although we cannot be absolutely certain, it seems highly probable that in the Q tradition we come closest to the actual words and actions of Jesus.

Q antedates the Gospels, and its themes of (1) redefining the Covenant community and (2) depicting Jesus as God's agent for the renewal of his people fit well the situation of first-century Judaism, as well as match impressively what we have seen to be the thrust of the earliest New Testament writings. The analysis of these themes follows this sequence.

The Privileges and Responsibilities of Discipleship in God's New People

Probably the best-known feature of Jesus' teachings is the collection known as the Beatitudes, in which he announces the ways in which God has blessed his faithful people. Instead of the more formal and more familiar version found in Matthew ("Blessed are the poor in spirit . . . ," Mt 5:3), Luke reports Jesus directly addressing his followers: "Blessed are *you* poor, for yours is the Kingdom of God" (Lk 6:20). In each of the Beatitudes in the Q form (as preserved in Luke) there is a contrast between the present and the future: Now is the time when the followers of Jesus are deprived and threatened; when God's Rule fully comes, they will be rewarded and vindicated for their faith and fidelity to Jesus (6:21–2). The joy they will experience on the day of God's delivering them from their present trials and difficulties links them with the prophets, who were persecuted by their unbelieving contemporaries but who will be vindicated by God in the future (6:23): "Blessed are you when men hate you, and when they exclude you and revile you and cast out your name as evil on account of the Son of Man. Rejoice in that day and leap for joy, for behold your reward is great in heaven; for so their fathers did to the prophets." Jesus and his followers stand in the tradition of the prophets of Israel, in that their declaration of God's message for his people is met with resistance and they find themselves shut out of society by its leaders.

The pattern of human values and social relationships that human beings have come to expect from one another and within themselves, Jesus now portrays as being overturned. The appropriate response to one's enemies and attackers is not retaliation but love. Jesus calls his followers to react in a way that completely surprises and disarms their opponents (6:27–35). God will reward those who are loving and merciful, since that is God's nature as well (6:36). Similarly, his followers are to avoid judging others, but instead are to be forgiving, as God is toward them (6:37). They are to be occupied with self-criticism, instead of denouncing others (6:41–2). It is not enough to hear Jesus' words: One must live by them, if one's life is to have a solid foundation that can survive the difficulties that lie ahead for the faithful (6:47–9).

Just as the standard patterns of response to others are challenged by Jesus, so he calls his followers to make a break with the one social unit from which they have gained their basic identity: the family. In contrast to wild animals, which have holes and nests where they share a common existence, Jesus calls those who are thinking of joining his movement to be prepared to leave their homes and to make a break in their obligations to parents and families. Even to take the time to honor a dead parent or to bid farewell to one's family has no place in the urgent role that Jesus foresees for those who follow him (Lk 9:57–62). Instead, one can expect fierce disagreement among the members of the family as a consequence of one's joining up with Jesus (Lk 12:49–56). The necessity of an absolute break with one's family is dramatically stated in Luke 14:26: "If any one comes to me and does not hate his own father and mother and wife and children and brothers and sister, yes, and even his own life, he cannot be my disciple." Some interpreters of Jesus' teachings have tried to blunt the force of this saying, by assuming that he is purposely overstating the case. But the clear point of these words is that commitment to the task for which Jesus is calling his disciples must take total priority over the nearly universal human pattern of family obligations.

The necessity to choose between competing sets of obligations is expressed in another way in Luke 16:13, where we read that no one can serve two masters. Human nature is such that one cannot live with divided loyalties. The choice is between total commitment to God and allowing one's life to be dominated by earthly possessions (that is, mammon, a Semitic word for wealth). The decision is made even more serious in Luke 14:27 where Jesus calls his followers to "take up the cross," which means in this case to accept so completely their responsibilities to him that they are prepared to meet their death on the cross, as he was so soon to do.

In addition to portraying the attitudes and values that are to characterize God's new people, Q includes the detailed instructions with which Jesus sent out his followers to spread his message and to perform the works of healing that are indications of the coming of God's Rule in which his followers and their hearers will find themselves (Lk 10:2–20). As important as the coming of the end of the age is (portrayed here as a harvest, with the disciples as workers in the harvest), there are only a small number who will share in this vital work (Lk 10:2). As they begin their mission in the name of Jesus, they are highly vulnerable to attack by those who oppose them and their message (Lk 10:3).

As they set out on their assigned task of preparing their hearers for the coming of God's Rule, they are not to make arrangements for even minimal monetary support for themselves. They are not to seek more comfortable accommodations as they move from village to village, but are to accept whatever food or hospitality is offered (Lk 10:5–8). Their message is to be that God's Rule is coming near (Lk 10:10); their works of healing and exorcism are to reinforce and demonstrate their message that the Kingdom of God is already manifesting itself through what Jesus said and did, and by extension, through what his followers are commissioned and empowered by him to do in his name. When a village scorns them or spurns their gospel, they are symbolically to shake the dust of that village from their feet. Yet this rejection in no way hinders the coming of God's Rule, although it calls forth the pronouncement of the coming of God's judgment as well (Lk 10:11–12). Q conveys the somewhat paradoxical view that although love and forgiveness are essential features of the nature of God, the divine offer of love is extended to all his creatures as an invitation rather than a coercion. Accordingly, the opportunity to hear and see the signs of the new age will be rejected by the Jewish cities and villages, while there is an open attitude toward the words and works of Jesus and his followers in such pagan centers as Tyre and Sidon (10:13–16).

What provides his followers the insight and courage to persevere in their role as messengers of the Kingdom is the assurance that through Jesus, God has disclosed to them his purpose. That plan has been hidden from those considered wise by the world at large, but it has been revealed to those whom the world regards as childlike, naive, innocent of worldly wisdom (10:21). Yet it is precisely to these that God's nature and plan for the creation have been made known. The agent of this revelation is Jesus, who here is reported as referring to himself simply as "the son" (Lk 10:22). Many in the past, including the prophets and kings of Israel, have sought to discern the divine purpose but have failed to do so. Now it has been made known through Jesus to his followers. This insight and responsibility can sustain them during the time of testing that will precede the end of the age.

The basic goal of this disclosure of God's plan for his people is given to the disciples in the prayer that Jesus teaches them, which is the Q version of what we know as the Lord's Prayer. It calls for the hallowing of God's name, which means the recognition by human beings of the nature and justice of God's plan for the world he has made. That awareness will be universal when God's Rule has fully come (Lk 11:2). Meanwhile, however, the followers of Jesus need a daily supply of food for their physical survival and of forgiveness, so that their relationship of faithful obedience to God may be sustained and their relationships to other members of God's people may be ever renewed. As humans, they might prefer to avoid the testing they will undergo before the new age comes (Lk 11:3–4). In keeping with the apocalyptic view of history, Jesus here simply assumes that God's people will go through a time of severe testing before the Kingdom comes in its fullness. They are to pray in confidence, therefore, that just as human parents seek to meet the needs of their children, so God will sustain them during the time of stress that will precede the coming of God's Rule (Lk 11:9–13). The attitude of forgiveness toward another member of the community is to be balanced by calling that erring person to account. Yet there is to be no limit to the willingness to forgive (Lk 17:3–4). Sustaining the members is the faith that God grants to them, and this can continue to increase (Lk 17:5–6).

In the Q tradition there is a series of important contrasts between the community of Jesus' followers and other groups. As in the writings of the Dead Sea community, those to whom these insights have been given consider themselves to be children of light, in contrast to the children of darkness, who cannot perceive what God is doing. The comparison between this divinely provided light, which illuminates the whole self, and the lamp is set out in Luke 11:33–6. The light is the symbol of the knowledge of God and his purpose. It is not an innate human capacity, but is given by God. The disciples who have received that light are encouraged to share it with others.

The most direct criticism of another group, however, is aimed at the Pharisees, with whom the early Christians had so much in common: Both were concerned to redefine participation in God's Covenant people; both worked at reinterpreting the Scriptures in order to understand God's purpose better; both met regularly for sharing insights and for table fellowship. The great difference between Jesus and the Pharisees lay in the insistence of the latter on ritual purity as the basis of participation, whereas Jesus welcomed all who sensed their need of divine grace and came to him and his followers in search of it. Jesus is described in Luke 11:39–52 as asserting that what God expects of his people is moral responsibility rather than the maintenance of ritual cleanliness. The values of the Pharisees include the desire to have their piety publicly recognized and admired (Lk 11:43), and the eagerness to make a reputation for themselves by their interpretations of the Jewish law. They honor the prophets as notables from the past, but do not honor them by paying heed to their criticism of the leaders of the nation (11:47–8). Jesus quotes the wisdom of God as announcing that messengers will be sent by God, and that they will be persecuted and killed. Indeed, the entire sweep of biblical history is characterized by the rejection of God's agents, from Genesis and the first murder (that of Abel, Gn 4:8) to the last book in the Jewish Bible in which Joash, the king, ordered the death of the prophet-priest Zechariah (2 Chr 24). It is in keeping with this tradition of rejecting God's messengers that the Pharisees, instead of using their study of the Scriptures as a way of understanding God's purpose for his people, have failed to gain this knowledge or to allow others to do so (Lk 11:52).

In some aspects of human experience, Jesus' opponents are able to discern what is going to happen. For instance, they can infer from present weather conditions what is likely to happen in the near future. But they cannot reason from what Jesus is doing and saying to the perception that the present order is coming to an end, and that God's new age is about to be established (Lk 12:54–6). Similarly, they have the good sense to come to terms with their accuser before they are dragged into court, but they do not have the ability to realize that God is about to call them to account, so that they must even now prepare themselves for the coming divine judgment.

In a series of vivid images, Jesus speaks in the Q tradition of the need to assess one's situation and to prepare for the im-

pending future crisis. One such illustration concerns a householder who refuses hospitality to a stranger who is at his door
seeking admission and food. The point of the parabolic utterance is that those who had been associated with Jesus during
his public career are going to claim a place as part of his family
or people in the future. But he denies their request and de-
nounces them as workers of iniquity. Those who will share in
the fellowship of the household of God include the founders
and agents of renewal of the Covenant people (Abraham, Isaac,
Jacob, the prophets), but not Jesus' self-contented, pious contemporaries. They will be "thrown out" (Lk 13:25–9).

Assurance is offered that there will be a future vindication of
Jesus as Son of Man (discussed under "Jesus' Role Contrasted
with John's"), although before that will come the period of rejection and suffering through which he and his followers must
pass. Meanwhile, however, the majority of those who think of
themselves as God's people will go about their daily responsibilities – marrying and giving in marriage, eating and drinking, buying and selling (Lk 17:22–7). None of these human
endeavors is wicked. But preoccupation with them betrays a
blindness to the more important factor: the impending divine
judgment and the establishment by God of his rule in the
world. As judgment fell on the careless and indifferent in the
stories of the patriarchs of ancient Israel, so it will fall on Jesus'
contemporaries, busy as they are with their own mundane affairs, and oblivious as they are to what God is in the process of
doing in this world. The price of sharing in this new order is the
willingness to give up one's own life in behalf of what God has
begun to achieve through Jesus (Lk 17:34). The result of this
dramatic divine intervention will be that human associations
will be shattered, and the unsuspecting will be aware of what
has occurred only when the vultures are swirling around the
carcasses of a bygone era (Lk 17:35–7).

Because the center of social existence for both the Pharisees and the Essenes of Qumran was table fellowship, and because both these groups regarded their common meals as a way of celebrating the presence of God in their midst, it is not surprising that these people would expect to share a glorious meal in the new age. Jesus' prediction of the blessedness of any who eat bread in the Kingdom of God (Lk 14:15) is presented in the gospel tradition as the occasion when Jesus utters a parable about the potential participants in that meal. Jesus is pictured in Q (as in the letters of Paul and the other gospel tradition) as sharing a similar hope: that the fellowship of the nucleus of God's people at the Last Supper would be renewed and fulfilled in the new age when God's purpose for his Covenant people would triumph. At issue between Jesus and his Jewish contemporaries is who is qualified to share in this fellowship meal of God's people. According to Q, the meal is compared with a special celebration, or banquet, for which advance preparations have been made, including widespread invitations. When the time for the banquet actually came, however, many of those invited were too busy with their own business and personal affairs to attend. Their excuses are indications of common sense: They must examine land or stock they are about to purchase. They must spend time with a new spouse (Lk 14:18–20). What is clear is that life as usual is taking priority for them over the new occasion of joy and fulfillment that is being provided for them through Jesus. The host of the banquet extends the invitation in two directions. First, he invites to his feast those who by ordinary social and religious standards would have been excluded from such affairs: the poor, the maimed, the blind, the lame. Religious law regarded such persons as unclean. We have noted that the Temple Scroll from the Dead Sea sect pronounced them to be unfit to enter the Temple of God in the new age. But the final phase of the invitation is even more radical. It is issued to those who are outside the city – that is, to those who are not part of the traditional people of

God (14:21–4). Those originally asked to take part in the banquet are ultimately excluded. One can readily imagine how objectionable this prediction would be to those who regarded themselves as the elect people of God. Jesus is not merely overturning their expectations; he is doing so in a way that claims that the purpose of God will be fulfilled through others than the Covenant people as the Jewish leaders have defined it.

Jesus as Revealer and Agent of God's Rule

The Preparatory Role of John the Baptist

The crucial role of Jesus in the working out of God's purpose for his people and for the creation is anticipated in the Q tradition about John the Baptist. John's challenging message is addressed to those who consider themselves to be children of Abraham (Lk 3:8). Yet his name for them is "offspring of snakes" (Lk 3:7). His intent is to warn them about the judgment that is to come when God brings the present order to an end and raises up a new people of God, in place of those who claim Abraham as their father, but who are no longer worthy of the convenantal relationship (Lk 3:9). Changing the image to that of harvesting grain, John foresees an outpouring of God's power (the Spirit) that will result in the judgment of the worthless and the preservation of the worthy (Lk 3:16–17).

Jesus Inaugurates the New Age

Yet John the Baptist appears in Q as the one who brings to a close the old era of the Law and the prophets. Jesus is the one through whom the good news is preached. It concerns the new age, but everyone who will enter that age must be prepared to endure conflict (Lk 16:16). Those who see in Jesus God's agent to bring in the new age are confident that all that had been predicted in the Scriptures will be fulfilled (Lk 16:17). When the turn of the ages comes, everything that has been hidden up to that point will be revealed. The purpose of God, which has been kept within the group of the followers of Jesus, will then be fully and publicly announced (Lk 12:2–3).

The Testing of Jesus' Followers

In spite of this prospect of conflict and suffering, the faithful messengers of Jesus are to be free of fear, since they are confident that God will vindicate them when the new age is fully come. God highly prizes them, just as he cares for all his creatures (Lk 12:4–7). The fate of everyone will be determined by their response to Jesus in the present age. In that day he will claim as his own those who have publicly acknowledged him, even at the risk of their own lives. Those who have denied him will be denounced by him in that day of bringing humanity to account (Lk 12:8–9).

Meanwhile, when his followers are brought before the religious and political authorities as a result of their associations with Jesus, he promises that the Spirit will give them instruction as to what to say in their defense (Lk 12:11–12). There is no way of predicting when that day of calling to account will come, any more than one can predict when a thief will enter one's house (Lk 12:39–40). All that his followers can do is to discharge as faithfully as possible the responsibilities that have been placed upon them in seeking to prepare their fellow humans for the coming of God's Rule. There is no excuse for those who assume that the crucial day of reckoning has been delayed. The master will punish any infidelity or any failure to meet one's obligations (Lk 12:44–6).

Jesus himself is the model of perseverance in a time of testing, as the Q traditions about his temptation show (Lk 4:3–12). The temptations this tradition relates are not urges to commit gross crimes or self-indulgent acts. Rather, they are suggestions by the tempter that Jesus use his extraordinary powers to show off his capabilities, such as changing stone into bread. Another temptation is to take a shortcut to the seat of authority, avoiding the suffering that he must undergo in God's plan, by acknowledging the Devil as his sovereign. The third temptation is to show that he can save his own life, by jumping unharmed from the pinnacle of the Temple, thereby demonstrating to the crowds of worshippers his amazing capacities. In each case, his response is to appeal to Scripture, in order to demonstrate where his sole reliance lies: on the power and purpose of God.

Jesus' Role Contrasted with John's

Of central significance in the Q material is the exchange between John the Baptist and Jesus, and Jesus' subsequent remarks about John (Lk 7:18–22). John had been placed in prison by Herod Antipas, the ruler of the district of Galilee, and heard there of the astonishing activities of Jesus. In order to find out from Jesus the meaning of his enterprise, John sent messengers to inquire of Jesus about the source and intent of his role. The response of Jesus was to call attention to the specifics of his miraculous works: The blind see, lepers are cleansed, the deaf hear, and the dead are raised up (Lk 7:22). This verse is composed of phrases from the prophecies of Isaiah (29:18–19; 35:5–6; 61:1). We have already noted that these forms of disability were seen as disqualifying one from full participation in the life of Israel, and especially from the formal worship of Israel's God. The prophecies were concerned with the renewal of God's people that would take place when the new age came. Jesus' answer to John clearly implies that the meaning of his acts is that this longed-for event is already beginning. But because it is taking place in defiance of the heightening of purity requirements going on at that time – of which John himself is a prime example – Jesus knows that John and others of his persuasion will be offended by his actions and the claims he is making for his work as the preparation for God's Rule (Lk 7:23).

But Jesus goes on to point out a further contrast between himself and John. The large crowds that had gone out into the barren land east of the Jordan to see and hear John the Baptist were drawn there, not by his unusual clothing, but by the power of his prophetic word of judgment on his Jewish contemporaries (Lk 7:24–6). Jesus makes the direct claim that John's role was the fulfillment of the prophecy of Malachi 3:1, where the prophet declares that God would send a "messenger of the covenant" to prepare the way "before *me.*" When Jesus quotes the verse, however, the pronoun is changed to "before *thy* face," and the reference is clearly to John as the one who prepares the way for *Jesus.* There is high praise for John ("among those born of women there is none greater," Lk 7:28), but John is seen as an outsider in comparison with those who are entering the Kingdom of God.

The people as a whole who had seen John at work were put off by his ascetic ways ("eating no bread and drinking no wine," Lk 7:33). But Jesus, who befriends those excluded by his pious contemporaries from a place among God's people ("tax collectors and sinners," Lk 7:34), is denounced by these same critics as a glutton and a drunkard. Clearly, by his open attitude toward those whose occupations or life-styles were considered by Jewish piety to be off limits, Jesus was both a shock and a threat to the religious establishment. The only justification for what Jesus is doing is the revelatory wisdom that his message and actions impart to those who have the divinely provided insight to recognize him as God's agent in establishing the New Covenant people (Lk 7:35).

These twin themes of the special disclosure of God's purpose to some, and his withholding of this understanding from those who consider themselves to be wise, are developed elsewhere

in Q as well (10:21–22). Jesus declares that it is the will of God
to reveal his plan to the innocent, the uneducated, those regarded by others as immature ("babies"), even while actively
concealing this knowledge from those considered wise by
human standards. But he goes on to assert who the distinctive
instrument of this revelation is: Jesus himself. Referring to
himself as "the Son," he announces that God alone knows who
he is, and that he alone knows God. All this understanding has
been given to him by God, and is passed on by Jesus to those to
whom he chooses to reveal it. To attain such knowledge is a
matter not of human achievement but of divine gift.

Jesus' special relationship to God is not depicted in the ab-
stract, however. Rather, it is evident to the eyes of faith in his
activities, and especially in his healings and exorcisms. The
pattern for his struggle with Satan in preparation for the coming of God's Rule is prepared for in the Q accounts of Jesus'
temptations (Lk 4:2b–12). Wherever the Kingdom of God is
preached, there will be violence resulting from his attack on
the powers of evil (16:16). In the Q version of the incident,
when Jesus' antagonists accuse him of performing his exorcisms through his alliance with Beelzebub, the prince of demons, he responds by claiming that when he casts out demons,
it is by the power granted him from God ("the finger of God"),
and that thereby God's Rule has already become a reality in
their midst. In the Q version of the parables of the mustard
seed and the growing tree (Lk 13:18–21), the point in each case
is that God's Rule is already a growing reality for those who
have eyes to see what God is doing through Jesus.

It is the very nature of God, as Jesus portrays him in the Q
tradition (Lk 15:4–7), to rejoice at the reconciliation to him of a
sinner, rather than to condemn the practice of Jesus and his
disciples of sharing fellowship with sinners, and inviting them
to participate in the new movement. As we noted earlier in this
chapter, Jesus represents himself in Q as the intermediary be-

tween God and his people: as Son, he alone knows the Father;
as revealer, he discloses God and his purpose only to those he
chooses (Lk 10:21–2). He also refers to himself in Q as "Son of
man," as when in Luke 7:33–5 he contrasts his attitude toward
sinners and those ritually excluded from God's people with the
ascetic demands made by John the Baptist. And in the process
of describing his own role, he identifies himself by this title.

The Range of Responses to Jesus

What is to be expected from the Jewish majority and from its
leaders is rejection of Jesus and his followers (Lk 11:49–50).
The irony is that the Jewish religious people continue formally
to honor the prophets, including treating their tombs as holy
places. And yet they have consistently ignored or rejected both
the message of the prophets and the prophets themselves. In
this vivid passage, Jesus says that the pattern of persecuting
and killing God's messengers was dominant throughout the
biblical period, which he epitomizes by reference to the first
and last murders described in the Bible: from Abel in Genesis
to Zechariah in the last book of the Hebrew canon (2 Chroni-
cles). Even while rejecting Jesus as a messenger from God, his
opponents demand of him a sign – that is, an indication in the
form of some extraordinary act or manifestation that God is
with him (Lk 11:29–32). Jesus flatly rejects the request, but he
reminds his opponents that the message from God conveyed by
Jonah and Solomon was received by pagans (the people of Nine-
veh, and the Queen of the South). And he predicts that these
people will stand up in the judgment day to condemn those
who have failed to recognize in Jesus the messenger from God.

Q assures the followers of Jesus that they will be vindicated
by God when the new age arrives, and that their role then will
include executing judgment on the twelve tribes of Israel –
presumably for their leaders' rejection of Jesus as God's agent

(Mt 19:28; Lk 22:28–30). Luke places this saying in the setting
of his account of the Last Supper, and uses the verb form that
corresponds to the Greek noun meaning "covenant" to testify
that God has promised him a ("covenanted") kingdom. This
language underscores the point that Jesus is not rejecting the
biblical claim of Covenant renewal in a new era, but is radically
redefining who the participants in that Covenant community
will be.

Covenantal Participation

Thus there is no story in the Q tradition of Jesus' trial and
execution, nor of the Resurrection, just as there is no account
of his birth. But Q clearly indicates Jesus' expectation that he
and his followers will suffer persecution and martyrdom, and
that God will act in the future to vindicate them against their
foes and to establish his kingdom, with themselves as central
actors in the new age of righteousness and peace. The sole
criterion for participation in this new people of God is to "acknowledge [Jesus] before other human beings" (Lk 12:8). The
negative counterpart of this public confession of Jesus is the
formal public denial of him, which Christians in the second
century were required to do by Roman imperial decree, under
penalty of death. It is possible – perhaps likely – that the
specific terminology used here in Q ("acknowledge/deny")
comes from the time after Jesus, but the underlying principle
seems to go back to Jesus himself. To associate publicly with
Jesus, who claimed to be agent and messenger of God, and who
redefined Covenant participation, could well lead to official
opposition and martyrdom at the hands of those who saw in
Jesus' challenge to his own religious tradition a profound threat
to the integrity of the Covenant people as it had come to be
defined in the Pharisaic tradition. Paul's confession in Galatians 1:13 that he had exceeded all his (Pharisaic) contempo-

raries in his persecution of the church and had sought to destroy it indicates that this interpretation of the gospel evidence is not implausible. Later developments, as we shall see, were to intensify the mutual antagonisms between emergent Christianity and rabbinic Judaism. The historical roots of this conflict are delineated for us in the pregospel tradition of Q, which very probably takes us back as close as we can come historically to the words and actions of Jesus. These themes derive from the twin challenges of Jesus to Jewish covenantal identity: his declaration concerning the inclusiveness of participation, and his justification of this policy on the ground of his role as God's agent to prepare his people for the Kingdom.

Chapter 4

What Can We Learn from Our Oldest Gospel?

As we have noted, Mark seems to be our oldest gospel and therefore provides us with our earliest narrative account of the career of Jesus. Although there is no indication within this Gospel as to who wrote it, from the early days of the church there was an effort to lend authority to this account of Jesus' career and teaching by linking it with one of the apostles. It is probably because Peter figures so prominently in Mark, and because in 1 Peter 5:13 Mark is referred to as Peter's "son," that this writing came to be attributed to Mark.

Mark's Literary Model

Was there a model for Mark to use in writing his gospel? In neither Jewish nor Greco-Roman literature of this period are there writings that resemble our Gospels in structure and strategy. There are biographies and an abundance of histories, but none combines the features of sketching the life of the central figure, giving summary reports of his teaching, and suggesting ways in which he was launching a movement. The closest analogy we have is from the Dead Sea Scrolls, in the writings known as the Scroll of the Rule and the Damascus Document, where the guidelines that are to shape the life and thought of the community are set in a framework that tells how the founder of the group was called by God and challenged to begin the work that gave rise to the new community. These writings are examples of what anthropologists call a "foundation document." Accordingly, we should expect the information about

Jesus in the Gospels not to be the report of a detached observer, but to be set in a framework of concerns for the aims and values of the community he called into being. And that is exactly the case.

Jesus' Human Origins

Although Mark portrays Jesus as standing in a unique relationship to God and possessing extraordinary powers, he reports his life in fully human terms. Jesus' birth is merely assumed, not described. His mother, brothers, and sisters are mentioned, with no hint of supernatural birth. There is no linking Jesus with Bethlehem, as in Matthew and Luke, and therefore no suggestion that he is of the royal house of David. In fact, Mark 12:35–7 seems to raise the question of how Jesus could be linked with traditional messianic hopes of Israel, since he is not of Davidic descent. When Jesus begins his public activity, he seems to have made a break with his family, moving from his tiny hometown of Nazareth in the Galilean hills to Capernaum, a larger town on the shores of the Sea of Galilee. Mark 2:1 simply pictures him as "at home" in Capernaum. It appears to have been a small one-room house with a packed dirt roof, of a type that can still be found in Palestinian villages. When friends bring a paralytic for Jesus to heal and cannot get to him because of the crowd, they dig through the roof and lower the man down in front of Jesus (Mk 2:1–4). Luke, who is accustomed to more elegant houses, reports that the friends "removed the tiles" (Lk 5:19) – tiles being the typical mode of roof construction in the wider Roman world.

Jesus' True Family

While Jesus is at home in Capernaum, crowds gather outside to see him perform another healing or exorcism. Among those assembled are some described in some translations as "his friends" (Mk 3:21). But it is clear from the outcome of the incident (3:31–5) that they are the members of his family who think he is crazy and want to get him out of the public view. Curiously, there is no mention of his father, Joseph. In Mark 6:3, Jesus is referred to as "the carpenter, the son of Mary." Perhaps Joseph had died by the time Jesus reached maturity, and so the fact that there was no father around when Jesus entered public life may have led to the charge that he was illegitimate. The names of his brothers are given and his sisters are mentioned, which implies that the family relationships are to be understood as normal.[1] Yet in Mark 3:35 he redefines the family as consisting, not of one's actual siblings, but of those who do the will of God – that is, as Jesus interprets it. In a society like that of the Jews, this dismissal of the actual family as the ground of one's identity is revolutionary in import, because family links back to the sons of Jacob, especially in the priestly line, were among the highest Jewish values. Yet Jesus redefines the family in this nongenealogical fashion, and does so in the name of God.

Jesus' Relationship to God and His Role in God's Purpose

Jesus' special relationship to God is portrayed by Mark in several ways that move beyond the claims in Q that focus on Jesus' special knowledge of God and his exercise of divine power (see Chapter 3, Jesus' Role Contrasted with John's). Following his

1. In some church traditions, which affirm that Mary was perpetually a virgin, it is assumed that the so-called brothers and sisters of Jesus were Joseph's children by a previous marriage. Mark, our oldest gospel, does not seem to imply this, nor does he indicate anything supernatural about the parentage of Jesus. It is in Matthew and Luke that the miracle of the Virgin Birth is set forth.

baptism by John, Jesus is reported as hearing a voice from heaven that identified him as the "Son of God" (Mk 1:11). At the time of his transfiguration in the presence of the inner circle of three of his disciples, the voice from the cloud declares, "This is my beloved son" (Mk 9:7). But Jesus immediately instructs the disciples not to disclose what they have seen and heard. Yet on the occasion of two exorcisms that he performed, the demons identify him as "Son of God" (3:11; 5:7), which indicates that the powers of evil recognize their enemy and his source of power.

This term, "Son of God," is used in the Old Testament to refer to both the people of God and to the king as their God-given leader. In Hosea 11, for example, the prophet describes Israel's escape from slavery in Egypt (the Exodus, as it is traditionally named) as God's calling "my son" out of Egypt. The point of the term "son" is not that the Israelites were supernaturally born, but that they stood in a special relationship to God's concerns and purpose. Similarly, in Psalm 2, the king of Israel is addressed as God's "son," with the declaration, "Today I have begotten you" – which refers to the day when the king is crowned. His role as "son" is that of one who rules over God's people by God's choice, through God's power, and in fulfillment of God's purpose. Because Mark gives no hint of the supernatural birth of Jesus as the basis of his divine sonship – and here Mark differs from Matthew and Luke, as we shall see – we must conclude that Son of God in Mark's tradition implies the specifying of Jesus' relationship with God, and of that unique purpose God is accomplishing through Jesus for his new people.

The title Jesus uses most often in Mark to refer to himself is "Son of Man," which we have seen to be used in the Q tradition. In Mark its connotations are more fully developed. In the Old Testament, this phrase is used to refer to human beings as the creatures of God: "What is man that thou art mindful of him, or the son of man that thou dost care for him?" is the question the psalmist raises in Psalm 8:4. His answer is to point to human beings as collectively the crown of God's created order, and as those to whom has been given responsibility to order and care for the creation as a whole (Ps 2:5–8). But the term is also used in Daniel 7:13, where God seizes control of the world from the evil powers that have ruled it, and gives it to "one like a son of man." The contrast is between the horrible beasts who represent the successive pagan empires and the human beings through whom God now reigns over creation. This contrast is made explicit in Daniel 7:17–18, where the beasts are identified with the wicked rulers, and those to whom the ultimate rule of God is given are called "the saints of the Most High." It is said of them (Dn 7:27) that "the kingdom and the dominion and the greatness of the kingdoms under the whole heaven shall be given to the people of the saints of the Most High; their kingdom shall be an everlasting kingdom, and all dominions shall serve and obey them."

As we saw to be the case with "Son of God," this term includes both (1) the concept of an agent through whom God establishes his rule, and (2) the people for and through whom that rule is maintained. In an apocalyptic Jewish writing from the first century A.D., the Similitudes of Enoch (which is quoted in Jude 14–15), Son of Man is used as a title for the agent of God. It is clear, therefore, that although "son of man" could be used to remind human beings of their human limitations, it was also understood by at least some within Judaism of this period as a designation for a person or persons through whom God's Rule would be established.

Jesus is reported by Mark as going beyond the perspective of Q, in that he uses "Son of Man" with three different dimensions of meaning. The first concerns his authority in setting the guidelines for the community of his followers. He does this in relationship to pronouncing the forgiveness of sins (Mk 2:10) and in setting aside the law prohibiting labor only when a good work is involved. But he declares himself to be Lord of the Sabbath. In both these instances, Jesus is engaged in a radical reinterpretation of how one qualifies for right relationship within the people of God.

The second dimension of the Son of Man role in Mark concerns Jesus' place in the achievement of God's purpose in the future. By the use of this title he is pictured as the final judge of all human beings (Mk 8:38), when those who abandon his cause will be abandoned by him. He announces that God will raise him from the dead, following his death at the hands of the religious authorities (9:9). Then in 13:26 and 14:62, Jesus is quoted as making the astounding claim that the religious authorities will see him coming in glory, vindicated by God, to gather his own faithful people from every corner of the earth. Some interpreters of Mark have tried to avoid the implications of these claims for Jesus' own self-awareness by suggesting that he was talking about someone else who would come at the end of the age. But the response of the authorities is not to denounce his sketch of the future, but to condemn him as a basic threat to the ideals and values of the Covenant people as the leaders define them.

Less surprising to modern readers, because Christian art and literature have tended to portray Jesus in his lowliness as "son of man," is the third use of this term in relation to his suffering and death. This perception is expressed in the form of a pattern of prediction in Mark 8:31; 9:31; 10:33–4 – verses that include both direct and indirect quotations of Jesus. But other statements about his impending death are made to his followers (9:12; 10:45), as well as to the authorities (14:21, 41). Although in Daniel it is obvious that Daniel and his friends are prepared to die rather than obey the decrees of the wicked king about what they eat and how they pray to their God, their death is not essential to their sharing in the kingdom that God is about to give them.

Jesus, as Mark depicts him, takes this matter a major step
further: It is necessary, in fulfillment of God's plan, that he
suffer and die as a sacrifice on behalf of others, in preparation
for the fulfillment of God's purpose for and through his people.
There is no real precedent for this astonishing claim in the
Judaism of this period, which makes more understandable why
the religious authorities could neither grasp nor agree to what
Jesus was proclaiming as God's final plan for his people. The
closest one can come to an understanding of the meaning of
Jesus' death is in the depiction of the suffering servant in Isaiah
52–3, where at times the servant seems to be the faithful
people and at times an agent who suffers on their behalf. Mark
10:45, where the title "Son of Man" is linked with serving, is
the closest the tradition comes to linking the triumphant Son
of Man and the suffering servant. Many scholars want to give
the early church credit for the combining of the triumphant
Son of Man and the suffering servant in its interpretation of
Jesus' death. But a verse like Mark 9:12, which links these two
roles implicitly and yet does not do so in the stylized form of
passages like 8:31, suggests that Jesus did indeed during his
lifetime come to terms with the increasing opposition that
confronted him from religious and political officialdom, and
that he developed a perspective in which his suffering would
find meaning in God's purpose for and through him.

From the outset of his public activity, however, his major
task was to announce and to help his contemporaries prepare
for the coming of the rule of God. Just as Israel was tested by
God in the desert before it was ready to enter the promised land
of Canaan, so Jesus is depicted by Mark as struggling with
God's adversary (that is, Satan) as he prepares for what Mark
sees as Jesus' God-given role. Unlike other prophetic figures
who spoke in general terms of the coming of the new age, Jesus
announces that God's Rule has drawn near. And in preparation
for the new era that God is about to establish, Jesus calls for
people to make a basic shift in their attitude and outlook. The

usual translation in the crucial verse, Mark 1:15, is "repent," which most people would understand as "to feel sorry for what one has done." What Jesus really calls for, however, is a change of mind, or as we might say, a change of heart. The reason for this call to a change of outlook is that the long-promised rule of God, as Jesus phrases it, has now drawn so near that its powers and transforming effects are already evident in what he does and in the new community he has begun to form.

The Privileges and Responsibilities of Discipleship

The radical nature of this change is apparent in the group that Jesus draws to himself as followers, or learners (which is what "disciples" means basically; Mk 1:16–20). As "fishers of men" they are to recruit into the new community a wide range of their fellow human beings. Jesus begins with a core of simple people, several of whom had the modest occupation of fishing. But among his followers was also one who represented a small group of Jews who would be despised and excluded from social relationships by nearly all other Jews: Levi, a tax collector. His Jewish name gives no hint of his livelihood, which would be seen by many of his Jewish contemporaries as a betrayal of his ethnic and religious heritage. He collected taxes for the Romans, who controlled the traditional land of Israel, and thus helped keep Palestine under gentile domination. Further, a major aspect of his tax collecting was the examination of and assignment of fees for transporting goods through the land; much of these materials would be ritually impure, and he as a Jew should not touch them. On both religious and nationalistic grounds, therefore, tax collectors were despised. Yet Jesus not only was cordial to Levi, but invited him to become one of his followers. Because the maintenance of ritual purity was one of the highest values among Jews in this period, and since sharing a meal with any nonobservant Jew was sure to result in defilement, Jesus defies these established rules by eating with Levi and other tax collectors and violators of the code of purity (2:13–17). Not only does Jesus engage in such violations, but he also defends what he is doing as a part of the divine commissioning for the task to which he has been called.

The simple qualities of the circle of twelve are given in Mark 3:13–19, although no two of the lists of disciples given in the gospels match exactly. Some of them have familiar Semitic names (Simon = Shimeon, James = Jacob, John = Jochanan), but others have Greek names [Andrew, Philip), which reminds the reader of Mark of the permeation of Galilee by Greek influences since the time of Alexander the Great in the fourth century B.C. The comment in Acts 4:13 about Peter and John that the authorities "perceived that they were uneducated, common men" is almost certainly quite accurate. Yet they, along with the rest of the twelve, are the ones to whom Jesus entrusts not only the spread of his message but also the exercise of the powers of healing and exorcisms that signify the drawing near of God's Rule (Mk 3:14).

This message of the inbreaking of God's Rule is presented by Mark not as a logical development of human thought or aspiration but as a God-given insight, reserved only for the members of the community. Intellectual capacities are not essential conditions for grasping the meaning of what Jesus preaches and performs. In Mark 4:10–12, Jesus declares that "the mystery of the Kingdom of God has been given to you [his circle of followers], but for those outside everything is in riddles [literally, parables]." There is a sharp division in Mark between those who see Jesus as God's agent for the establishment of his kingdom, and those who do not. The latter include those who are occupied with their own affairs, as well as those who see in him a threat to the present political, social, and religious order. It is these who will "see but not perceive," who will "hear but not understand."

A major factor in the inability of many of Jesus' hearers to accept what he claims is that what he describes is in conflict with common wisdom. A common point of the parables reported in Mark 4 is that there is a major difference between the small beginnings of certain undertakings and the vast outcomes. For example, the mixed or even fruitless results of the effort of the farmer sowing seed on a variety of soils are in sharp contrast with the astonishingly rich harvest that comes – up to a hundredfold (4:1–9). The very growth of the seed, through its own inner forces and apart from human observation, leads to the rewarding harvest (4:26–9). Similarly, the Parable of the Mustard Seed contrasts the smallest of seeds with the largest of shrubs that it ultimately produces (4:30–2). All three of these little parables point to the seemingly limited, unauthorized, and initially unnoticed work that Jesus began, in calling into his fellowship these co-workers to announce the coming of God's Rule, and to manifest its inbreaking through the healings and exorcisms that they perform. At the outset of his public career, no casual observer would have suspected for a moment that the results of his work would be in conflict with the authorities in Jerusalem, to say nothing of the outcome that Jesus is reported as announcing: In the new age, God's new people will be gathered "from the four winds, from the ends of the earth" (Mk 13:27).

In reporting the teachings of Jesus – in this case, the parables – Mark includes material that seems to be more appropriate in the life of the early church than in the time of Jesus. That should not be surprising, since the gospel tradition was preserved because of its ongoing relevance for the people who became followers of Christ through the testimony of the disciples and of others who originally followed Jesus. In Mark 4:13–20 there is an elaborate explanation of the Parable of the Sower. Each element of the parable is given an explanation by comparing it with some feature of the early church. The sower is the preacher. The seed he sows is the Christian message, or "word." The various hearers of the gospel are compared with different types of soil, although in the process of this allegorical explanation, the hearers are identified as the seed that does, or does not, bear fruit. The thorns that hinder the growth of faith are said to be "the cares of this age," "delight in riches," "desire for things." Although it can be imagined that such temptations would be alive among Jesus' original circle of followers, it seems more likely that these problems have arisen after the church is more established and includes the wealthier classes. The interpretation of the parable is the Markan community's way of showing the relevance of Jesus' teaching for their own time.

The Mounting Hostility toward Jesus

Even the public evidence of his extraordinary powers in word and act produces mixed reactions among Jesus' contemporaries. The crowds gather to see what he can do (Mk 1:28, 32, 37, 45; 2:2, 13; 3:7, 19, 32; 4:1, 36; 5:21; 6:33–4). Amazement is expressed that one who came from such humble origins ("the carpenter," 6:3) possesses such abilities. Yet the general reaction seems to be one of unbelief, to which Jesus responds with amazement and with the observation that "a prophet is not without honor, except in his own country" (6:4–6). The reaction of the religious leaders and those allied with the political authorities is more serious, however. Mark tells us that when Jesus had performed a healing on the Sabbath and defended his violation of the Sabbath law, "The Pharisees went out, and immediately held counsel with the Herodians [members of the court of Herod Antipas, or of his family] against him, how to destroy him" (3:6). These groups would not have had much in common, since the Pharisees were mainly concerned with the maintenance of strict ritual purity, whereas the Herodians were committed to keeping in power the descendant of Herod the Great, who governed the province of Galilee on behalf of the pagan Roman Empire. But for both groups, Jesus was a threat to established order.

As we have noted, the major basis for Jesus' popular appeal is said by Mark to have been his healings and exorcisms. In our analysis of the Q sources, we saw that Jesus identified his casting out of demons as a sign that by God's power ("the finger of God") he was able to do these acts that brought God's Rule into the midst of the throngs that followed him. In Mark 3:23–7, he associates his exorcistic activity with the defeat of Satan, who in the Jewish thinking of that time was the primary agent of evil and who had seized control of the universe and its inhabitants in defiance of God's purpose for the Creation. Contrary to the accusation of Jesus' critics, he is not in league with the power of evil – by whatever designation he is known: the Devil, Satan, or Beelzebub – but is instead God's agent for his defeat. Even now, by his exorcisms, he is seizing control from Satan, or as he phrases it in Mark 3:27, binding the strong man so that he may "plunder his house."

Two aspects of Jesus' activity as Mark presents them were viewed by the Jews as threatening or actually violating the integrity of the Covenant people. One was Jesus' setting aside some of the basic laws, such as abstinence from work on the Sabbath. The other was his defying the purity laws, and claiming to do so in the interest of work that God had given him to do. We must look at each aspect of this threat to the Jewish standards that Mark recounts Jesus as posing and defending.

Mark 2:23–8 recounts the story of Jesus' disciples helping themselves to some grain as they passed through a field on the Sabbath, and then rubbing off the husk and eating it. The Law required farmers to leave some grain unharvested in the fields for the benefit of the poor. But as religious persons, the disciples should have known that picking and rubbing the grain was prohibited on the Sabbath. Not only does Jesus not condemn their actions, but he appeals to a precedent from the Jewish

Bible, in which David was given sacred bread to eat that was unlawful food for him and his associates, as nonpriests (1 Samuel 21:1–7).

Two stories of Jesus' astonishing powers are linked in Mark 5:21–43. In the first of these, an official of the synagogue urges Jesus to come home with him in order to heal his daughter, who is near death. Jesus is delayed by a woman with a bloody discharge who came up behind him and touched his cloak (5:27) and was instantly cured of her ailment. Jesus' only reported words to her were "go in peace, and be healed" (5:34). On reaching the house of Jairus, the synagogue official, Jesus learns that the child has already died. But going in to her with the family alone, he touches her, speaks to her (in Aramaic), and she is restored to life (5:40–3). What is remarkable in these stories is not only that Jesus has the power to heal and to restore to life, but that in doing such work he simply ignores the strict legal prohibitions then operative in Judaism against having physical contact with the sick or the dead. To touch them or to be touched by them was to become ritually polluted. Yet in both these stories, Jesus is depicted as meeting the needs of the ailing, with no attention to the ritual problems involved.

Jesus' preaching, healing, and performing exorcisms among those regarded as ritually impure are said by Mark to have been carried further by his disciples. Thus, in 6:6–13, they are commissioned to go from village to village, healing, casting out demons, and preaching, just as Jesus has done and by his authority. The boy who has seizures as a result of possession by a demon cannot be healed by the disciples. But at Jesus' command, the demon is expelled and the boy is cured. Even though the boy appears to be dead, Jesus is described as reaching out to touch him – once more in defiance of the ritual purity traditions (9:14–27). The failure of the disciples to cure the boy is said to be the result of their failure in prayer (9:28–9).

Jesus' setting aside the dietary and other ritual laws is evident throughout Mark. We have already noted his sharing table fellowship with those who were ritually impure. But in Mark 7:1–23 he is reported as rejecting the very notion of maintaining ritual purity in connection with the preparation and eating of food. The Pharisees' expansion and elaboration of the Jewish law of purity had included requiring obedience at meals eaten in the home to the regulations set down in the Bible for the priests in the central sanctuary of Israel. Jesus' challenge to his critics includes not only applying to them the criticism uttered by Isaiah to those who professed to honor God while in fact following their own rules (Mk 7:6–7; cf. Is 29:13), but he goes on to deny the whole principle of ritual defilement.

The example he offers of their evasion of their clear responsibility is the contrast between the commandment to honor one's parents (Ex 20:12, 21:17; Dt 5:16; Lv 20:9), which they profess to obey, and their actual practice of saying that they have dedicated everything to God and thus have nothing left with which to take care of their parents (7:11–12). This is followed by the flat declaration that "there is nothing outside a human being which by going into him can defile him" (7:15). This is then elaborated and made specific in 7:18–23, in what is described as a private explanation to his followers. True defilement comes from the human heart: "evil thoughts, fornication, theft, murder, adultery, coveting, wickedness, deceit, licentiousness, envy, slander, pride, foolishness" (7:21–2). It is important to note that while some of these are outward actions, many of them are inner attitudes, which cannot be legislated or punished and hence are beyond the scope of ritual or performance code.

This kind of challenge laid down by Jesus in the Markan tradition is radical and profound. Jesus is here calling into question the very principles and procedures by which Israel had come to gain and maintain its special identity as the Covenant people. The principles were operative among Jews of vari-

ous persuasions: the Sadducees and the priests, as well as the
Pharisees and the Dead Sea community. If Jesus had merely
rejected these purity principles, he could have been dismissed
by the religious leaders as a crackpot or a spoiler. But he does
so, in this tradition, by claiming divine support for his point of
view, and by appealing to the precedent of the prophets and
leaders of ancient Israel, including direct quotations from
Scripture. The fact that he is attracting a wider popular following constitutes a real threat, not only to the official leaders, but
to the integrity of the Jewish people as well.

Closely linked with this challenge to Jewish identity is the
pattern of outreach by Jesus to those on the fringes or wholly
outside the people of Israel. Among those who are depicted as
joining the multitude by the Sea of Galilee are not only those
from Jewish territory (Galilee, Jerusalem, Judea), but also those
from gentile districts: Idumea (the ancient land of the Edomites)
and other districts east of the Jordan, where the successors of
Alexander the Great had built Hellenistic cities completely
equipped with pagan temples, theaters, baths, and gymnasia;
and Tyre and Sidon, centers of Hellenistic culture to the north of
the land of Israel. In Mark 5, Jesus crosses over into this gentile
territory and carries on the same kinds of activities there that he
had in Jewish districts. Gerasa was one of these Greco-Roman-
style cities set down in the Middle East. The presence outside
Gerasa of a "great herd of swine" shows that it is not Jewish
territory. Jesus does not merely associate with the inhabitants,
but gives special attention to one who is living in a tomb (5:2–3)
– which would have put him off limits to any purity-conscious
Jew. Through this man's report of what God had done for him
through Jesus (5:19), the story of Jesus is now being proclaimed
in this group of Greek-style cities, the Decapolis (5:20).

The precedent of reaching out into gentile territory is confirmed, according to Mark (7:24–37), by Jesus' tour of preaching
and healing in Tyre and Sidon. This venture outside predomi-

nantly Jewish territory is mentioned in Q, but Mark also reports that Jesus carried on his work in the Decapolis. There probably were ritually observant Jews living in these places, but the only contact Mark reports Jesus as making in this pagan district is his expelling the demon from a child in response to the urgent request of her gentile mother (7:26, 30).

Redefining Covenantal Participation

It seems likely that Mark does not intend to report Jesus' activities in gentile territory as an exception to Jesus' normal range of associations, but that he wants to convey to the reader of his time that the Jesus movement is as open to Gentiles as to Jews. In elaborately symbolic form, Mark 6:30–44 describes Jesus as feeding with supernaturally provided bread the crowd that follows him, just as Moses had been God's instrument for feeding the hungry people of Israel in the desert of Sinai (Ex 16). As a symbolic reference to the number of the tribes of Israel, Mark reports that there were twelve baskets full of fragments left over after the meal in which all were fed. The symbolism of Mark's story points in another direction as well, in that he depicts Jesus as using technical language at the meal establishing the New Covenant: "He took, he blessed, he broke, he gave" (Mk 14:22). In 8:1–10, however, Mark tells a similar story, but instead of five thousand (Mk 6:44), there are four thousand (8:9). And instead of twelve baskets of remains, there are seven – which was the symbolic number in Acts 6 for the leaders of the gentile wing of the early church. It is impossible to determine what historical material lies behind these two narratives of the miraculous feeding, but the symbolic significance for an inclusive Covenant community is fully clear. Both Jews and Gentiles have a potential place in the ranks of God's new people.

Comparable to Jesus' redefining the terms for Covenant par-

ticipation are his challenges to the accepted interpretations of
various aspects of the Jewish religious and social institutions of
his time. In the biblical traditions, there was explicit provision
for a husband to divorce his wife, as Jesus recalls when ques-
tioned on the subject (Mk 1:1–12; cf. Dt 24:1). The issue at that
time was, what was sufficient grounds for divorcing one's wife?
Did the biblical condition – finding something unclean or in-
decent in her – imply that she had been unfaithful? Or did it
refer to some ritual failure or defiling ailment on her part? Or
did it give the husband an easy excuse to get rid of someone
whom he now found to be offensive? The Jewish interpreters of
the time debated these issues, according to later rabbinic traditions. But Jesus appeals behind the legal provision for divorce
to the divine intention in creating humans as male and female:
that they were to be joined as one (Gn 2:24). And he adds that
no one should separate what God has joined. In the private
explanation that follows (and we have come to see that Mark
uses this pattern frequently in his portrait of Jesus in relation
to his followers), Jesus says that for man or woman to divorce
and remarry is to commit adultery (10:12). Some scholars have
claimed that this could not be an authentic saying of Jesus
because Jewish law made no provision for a woman to divorce
her husband. What seems more likely, however, is that this
decree of Jesus is part of his radical reinterpretation of Covenant obligations for God's people.

  As his account moves toward the climax of Jesus' confronta-
tion with the authorities in Jerusalem, Mark concentrates on
the issues between Jesus and the religious leaders of his day
(Mk 10–13). One of these concerns the place children are to
have within the Covenant people. Although nearly all the evidence about the development of the synagogue is from after the
time of Jesus, it seems very likely that in its beginnings the
synagogue was a "gathering" (as the term itself implies) of
adult Jewish males. Jesus, by contrast, welcomes children and

declares that the child's attitude of ready acceptance of what is offered is a model of how people should receive the Kingdom of God: as a gift (10:13–16). The description of Jesus as taking the children, blessing them, and laying his hands upon them may have set the pattern for the church's formal dedication of children through infant baptism, but it may also be an indication that the church's subsequent practice came to be attributed to Jesus. The basic principle of receiving children into the new community seems clearly to go back to Jesus in any case.

In most cultural or religious settings, the fact that one has many possessions is taken as a sign of divine approval and favor. The rich young man who inquires about gaining life in the age to come (10:17–31) is also confident of his moral qualities, as gauged by his obedience to the commandments (Ex 20:12–16; Dt 5:16–20). Jesus, moved by this man's earnestness and concern, tells him to part with all that he has. At that point, the young man departs in sorrow because of the "great possessions" that he has been told to give to the poor. Jesus emphasizes to his followers how hard it is to give up one's worldly goods, comparing it to the unlikely event of an awkward, ungainly camel crawling through the eye of a needle (10:25). But he also commends his disciples, who, having given up the security of family and family possessions, will be rewarded many times over in the life of the age to come (10:29–31). A similar point is made in 12:41–4, where Jesus rates the poor widow's contribution to the temple of two copper coins as more significant than the showy gifts of the wealthy. In both these stories his advice flies in the face of common wisdom concerning the assurance of one's moral qualities that comes with wealth.

Because there was no basis in the first five books of the Bible for belief in resurrection, the Sadducees did not accept that notion and ridiculed those who did (Mk 12:18–27). They tried to make the point that it was a foolish idea by recalling the provision in the law that said that when a man died, his brother was to marry the widow in order to raise up children for the dead man (Dt 25:5–6). If there is a resurrection, they say, then in cases where a woman has been married to a succession of brothers, in the new age it will be impossible to decide whose wife she is. Jesus' response is to point out that all God's people have the same relationship to him, regardless of the generation or time in which they live. The implication is that in the new age human relationships are not merely continued as they are experienced in this life, but are transformed.

Which is the most important of the commandments? This was an issue that occupied successive generations of rabbis from the later first century on. Here Mark pictures Jesus as in agreement with one of the scribes. At this point in the history of Judaism, scribes (literally, "book people") were those who devoted their lives to the study and interpretation of the Scriptures. As students of the Bible, they fulfilled some roles roughly comparable to those of modern lawyers, as well as of clergy and professional counselors. Whether at this stage in Jewish history they were amateurs or paid professionals is impossible to determine. In Mark's account of the interchange (12:28–34), Jesus combines three crucial and basic elements of Jewish convictions: (1) the so-called *shema* – "Hear, O Israel . . ." – from Deuteronomy 6:4; (2) the commandment to love God, which follows the *shema*; and (3) the call to love one's neighbor as oneself (Lv 19:18). The scribe not only agrees with Jesus' formulation of the basic human moral obligation, but adds the factor (based on Samuel's words to the disobedient King Saul in 1 Sm 15:22) that obedience to these requirements is more important than the offering of sacrifices in the cultic system. The implicit challenge to the significance of the sacrificial system is spelled out later in Mark's portrait of Jesus (Mk 13).

Redefining the Messiah and His People

The major emphasis throughout Mark – especially from Mark 7 to the end – is the challenge Jesus represented to the major norms of behavior and expectations effective in Judaism in the first century of our era. There was no single way in which the coming of the Messiah was understood, as we have observed in our analysis of Q (see Chapter 3, Jesus' Role Contrasted with John's) and earlier in this chapter. Although in Jewish tradition the faithful community was warned about the likelihood of persecution or martyrdom before the final deliverance would come, there was no developed notion that the Messiah himself must suffer.

It is not surprising, therefore, that Peter and the other disciples could not grasp Jesus' predictions that he "must" suffer in order to fulfill his God-given task of establishing the New Covenant people. As Mark reports, Peter rejects the notion outright (Mark 8:32) and is rebuked by Jesus in return as the instrument of Satan. Following the second formal announcement by Jesus of his suffering and death, the disciples bicker among themselves as to who will be the greatest within the new community (9:34). Jesus responds by warning them that his followers must accept the role of servant on behalf of others (9:35–6). The third and fullest prediction of his crucifixion and resurrection (10:33–4) is followed by a contest between James and John, to see who will have the place of honor in the Kingdom of God. And once more, Jesus reminds them of the servant role, which he is about to fulfill on their behalf and for the sake of God's new people (10:35–45). Although in their present form these announcements of his death and resurrection probably are formulations from the early church, they very likely reflect two important historical factors: that Jesus came to see that his death was essential to fulfilling his divinely assigned role, and that this notion was in tension with the various forms of messianic expectation that were alive in Israel in his day.

The same conflict between the popular messianic notions of the triumphant agent of God who defeats his enemies through the exercise of power and Jesus' understanding of his role is apparent in the story of the so-called Triumphal Entry into Jerusalem (Mk 11:1–10). Mark does not report that Jesus rides in as a king, but only that in some way his entry is linked with the coming of God's awaited rule. The shout of the crowd recalls Psalm 118:25–6, where the blessedness is pronounced of the one who enters (Jerusalem? the Temple?) in the "name of the Lord" – that is, with God's authority and in fulfillment of his purpose. The spreading of garments and branches in Jesus' path recalls this same passage from Psalm 118. The fact that he comes on an ass, rather than on an impressive horse, is significant as well. The allusion is to Zechariah 9:9, where the victorious king comes in peace and humility. Anyone who has seen a Middle Eastern donkey knows that no one can be impressive mounted on such a humble beast, short of stature as it is and head hanging down. Once more, the choice of this mode of entrance into the city – the first that Mark has reported of Jesus – is significant: His role does not fit that of those expecting a military or forceful takeover of power from Rome.

Those who might have expected direct action on the part of Jesus were disappointed. Mark (unlike Matthew and Luke, who report his going into the Temple and taking control there) simply says that Jesus entered the Temple, looked around, and left (11:11). But this is followed by a description of an unfruitful fig tree (11:12–14), which recalls the image found in the prophets (e.g., Jer 8:13–15) of Israel as morally unproductive and therefore subject to divine judgment. God's rebuke of the disobedient people is symbolized by the withering of the tree, which is subsequently described (Mk 11:20–1).

It is in this setting that Mark places Jesus' attack on the scribes as pious show-offs (12:37–40) who draw attention to themselves by their long robes and seek places of special honor in the gathering of worshippers in the synagogue. His criticism of them is that they live by taking advantage of the weak, and try to cover up their deceits by long-winded prayers. Although they claim to be interpreters of God's will for his people, they are destined for severe divine judgment. Significantly, Luke and Matthew (especially the latter) greatly expand this aspect of the Jesus tradition. They were writing after the fall of Jerusalem, as we shall note later in this chapter and in Chapter 5, at a time when the mutual hostility between Jews and Christians had built up considerably.

Another issue that Jesus addresses is one that was increasingly serious for Jews in the latter third of the first century and the early decades of the second century: What attitude should be taken toward the domination of Palestine by the Romans? The priests and their allies, the Sadducees, received imperial approval for their role in operating the ritual activities in the Temple and participated in the local council, which was given some degree of autonomy in the regulation of life in Judea. They were apparently content to work with the Romans, and sought no overturn of power. The Pharisees had shifted their attention from politics (in which they had earlier been vigorously engaged during the days of the Jewish monarchs who were descendants of the Maccabees) to the development of personal and group piety through the voluntary gathering of Jews for prayer and study of the Bible in their homes. To this way of life Rome offered no threat. And the maintenance of a stable government and economy gave the Pharisees the assurance that their form of religion could continue unchallenged. The Essenes had withdrawn to the Dead Sea settlement, where they were awaiting divine intervention to expel the Romans as well as the Jerusalem-based Jewish authorities, after which they would be placed in power by God's direct action. Meanwhile, however, they made no move toward insurrection against Rome.

Yet behind all these positions, which acquiesced in the powerful presence of Rome, there was a resentment of being controlled by a pagan power. The motivation for the question raised by the coalition of Pharisees and Herodians (12:13–17) was to require Jesus to take a public stand on this touchy issue. If he came out for an uprising against Rome, then they could report him to the Romans as a revolutionary. His response (12:17) was to throw back on his questioners the obligation to decide how they were to meet their responsibilities to the occupying power, Rome, and to God. There is no hint of a move toward political revolt in Jesus' words, and yet there is a message of a higher priority than the obligation of paying taxes to Caesar.

The most serious challenge to his Jewish contemporaries that Mark reports Jesus as raising concerned Israel's unique role in the purpose of God. This is evident in two major ways in the later part of Mark. The first of these is embodied in the Parable of the Wicked Tenants (12:1–12). The parable builds on the imagery of Isaiah 5, where the ways that an owner deals with his unproductive vineyard are an allegory of God's actions toward his Covenant people. The same image is used by other prophets as well (Hos 10:1; Jer 2:21; Ez 19:10–14). The parable in Isaiah tells how the owner made every provision for the fruitfulness of the vines, and yet all the vineyard produced was wild grapes (Is 5:4). As a result, the owner broke down its boundaries, made it a waste, and stopped both the workers from tending it and the rain from falling on it.

Adapting this imagery, Jesus tells of an absentee owner of a vineyard, who let it out to tenants and left the country. When he later sent servants to collect his profit from the vineyard operation, the tenants mistreated them, even going to the extreme of killing some of the messengers (12:5). When the

owner's son came, they killed him as well, hoping thereby to
obtain the vineyard for themselves. What will be the owner's
reaction to this perversion of his purpose? "He will come and
destroy the tenants and give the vineyard to others" (12:9). The
rejection of the son is to be understood through Psalm 118:22–
3, which announces that what humans have rejected, God will
use as the cornerstone of his new undertaking. Since the basic
image of the parable concerns the destiny of Israel, the point is
clear: God through Jesus is establishing a New Covenant
people. Mark leaves no doubt as to how this parable was received by the religious leaders: "They perceived that he had
told the parable against them" (12:12).

Jesus Confronts the Authorities in Jerusalem

According to Mark, the other major challenge to Israel's understanding of itself in God's purpose for his creation concerns the
Temple. Regarded by all Jews as the special place where God
was present among his people, the Temple was at the same
time the chief source of income for Jerusalem and Judea, the
chief attraction for tourists, and the major source of pride for
Jews as a result of Herod's splendid rebuilding of the Temple.
This had begun in the decades before the birth of Jesus, and
while impressive to the most sophisticated visitor, the Temple
complex was not yet complete in detail when it was destroyed
by the Romans in A.D. 70 as retaliation for the Jewish na-
tionalist revolt. Yet most important for Jews, the Temple was
where God could be approached by his people, whether in grati-
tude or penitence. By the faithful observance of the annual
round of sacrifices and ceremonies there, Jews believed that
they assured God's fidelity to his people, to their crops, and to
their posterity. In the most literal sense, it was by visiting the
Temple that the people of Israel drew near to God.

In approaching God, only the high priest could enter the

inner sanctuary, the Holy of Holies, and only in preparation for
the Day of Atonement and with the appropriate sacrifices. A
larger inner structure, the Holy Place, was accessible to the
priests on other sacred occasions, however, and the Court of
Israel was open to all male Israelites. Women could go only so
far as the Court of Women, and Gentiles were limited to the
outer courts, which were known as the Court of the Gentiles
(or Nations). This latter was by far the largest area in the Temple complex, and was the place where non-Jewish tourists
could come to see this famous building, and where merchants
and money changers made available the sacrifices and coinage
that worshippers needed to fulfill their obligations as God's
Covenant people. Jesus protests that what had been intended as
the place where the Gentiles could approach the God of Israel
is now a place of commerce (11:17).

Jesus responds to the amazement of his disciples on entering
the Temple and seeing the splendor of the structure by predicting that it will be utterly destroyed (13:1–4). In one of Mark's
characteristic private explanation scenes, Jesus tells the disciples about the dire difficulties that his followers and all the
faithful will pass through at the end of the present age. The
Temple will be made to serve as a pagan shrine, as it had been
two centuries earlier by the pagan ruler, Antiochus Epiphanes.
In 168 B.C. he had ordered that a statue of himself as Zeus be
erected in the Jerusalem Temple, and that all his Jewish sub-
jects should honor him there accordingly. This had triggered
the Maccabean Revolt, which resulted in the rededication of
the temple in 165. Similarly, the Roman emperor Caligula
(reigned 37–41) had also decreed that his statue be set up there,
but he was assassinated before his decree was carried out. Jesus
is portrayed as expecting something similar to this to happen
once more, but this time the result will be the scattering of the
people of God and the utter ruin of the Temple. That will be
followed by the triumphant appearance of the Son of Man

(13:24–7). Yet God will preserve his scattered new people, in spite of the difficulties they must undergo (13:19–20). The speech – which is the longest consecutive set of sayings in Mark – ends with the word that no one can know when this will take place, but that everyone must be ready. The section ends with a parable of an absent householder, whose servants must be ready for his return at any time (13:33–7). This part of Mark (Chapter 13) has been considered by many scholars as the creation of the early church, written just prior to, or at the time of the impending fall of Jerusalem (in 66–70) and the destruction of the Temple. The theory is that they regarded this catastrophe as God's final act of judgment on traditional Israel before the new age arrived. The fact that Matthew and Luke have expanded this material, however, and made it more explicit in its predictions of the coming of the Roman army (as we shall see when we examine the Gospel of Luke), suggests that there may well be at least a core of material here that dates back to Jesus. The basic announcement of the destruction of the Temple and of the subsequent gathering of God's new faithful people seem to have originated with Jesus, however. His having made these predictions was very likely a major factor in the formation of the coalition of religious leaders who sought to get rid of him.

Jesus' final time with his disciples, as Mark describes it, is the familiar last meal, with its major focus on the bread and wine that are shared. The plot has formed to destroy Jesus (14:1–2), and to do so with as little notice as possible by the crowds gathered in Jerusalem for the celebration of the Passover. Jesus is pictured as defying the purity laws by staying at the home of a leper, where a discerning woman anoints him for his impending death (14:3–9). The betrayal of Jesus to the authorities by Judas is planned (14:10–11) and carried out (14:43–52) when the armed group sent by the priests, scribes, and other leaders seizes Jesus while he is outside the city with his

disciples in Gethsemane. The meal is designated by Mark as a
Passover, the festival in which the Old Covenant people celebrated their founding through God's deliverance of Israel from
slavery in Egypt. But there is no mention of the lamb or the
bitter herbs that were essential elements in that Jewish tradition. Instead, there is an account of the shared loaf and cup,
which symbolize Jesus' giving of himself and of his life, respec-
tively. The blood of the Covenant (Paul's version of this tradition adds "New Covenant," 1 Cor 11:23–5) is poured out on
behalf of all his followers. The Covenant will fulfill its divinely
intended aims when the Kingdom of God has fully come (Mk
14:22–5). Jesus' role as founder and leader of the new people of
God is depicted by his reference to the shepherd and the sheep
– an allusion to Zechariah 13:7 (Mk 14:26–31). Peter's denial of
Jesus and the disciples' flight when Jesus is seized confirm the
picture that even his closest followers do not yet understand
what God is doing through him on their behalf. He does, however, predict that they will be regathered in Galilee after God
has raised him from the dead (14:28). He continues in prayer,
struggling over the divinely given role of suffering that he is
soon to enter (14:32–42).

Taken captive, Jesus is given a hearing by the council, or
Synedrion (which is later transliterated into Hebrew as Sanhe-
drin). This consisted of local Jewish leaders and was given responsibilities for supervising the common life of the inhabitants of the region of Jerusalem and Judea, as was Roman
practice everywhere. Under direct questioning before this re-
gional council, Jesus claims to be the Messiah and promises
that God will exalt him as Son of Man in the new age (14:61–2).
Yet the Jewish authorities cannot decide what to do with him,
and so turn him over to the political authority, Pilate. The
Roman governor then sentences him to death as a claimant to
the Jewish throne, and ironically releases for the Jews an insur-
rectionist (15:7). The inscription placed above Jesus' head as he

is lifted up on the cross confirms that he is dying on a political, anti-Roman charge, rather than as a violator of Jewish law. Jews were given authority to execute those guilty of capital crimes as defined by their religious laws, but that right was not exercised in Jesus' case. The mockery that he receives on the cross confirms the political charge that he sought to be "king of the Jews" (15:26, 32). With a deeply human cry of divine questioning, quoted from Psalm 22:1, Jesus dies (15:33–41). A Roman officer at the site of his death acclaims him as "son of God" (15:39), and a pious Jewish leader takes responsibility for burying him quickly before the Sabbath begins (15:42–7). Two women named Mary see where he was buried, and plan to return at dawn following the close of the Sabbath, in order to prepare his body for proper burial.

When they do return (16:1–8), the tomb is open and the body is gone. A young man reminds them of Jesus' word to Peter and the disciples that they would see him in Galilee after God had raised him from the dead. Mark ends his account with that event not yet described, and accordingly the followers of Jesus are filled with fear as they await the outcome. The other gospel writers do not end the story at this point, but describe in detail either Jesus' appearance at the empty tomb or his subsequent appearances to his followers or both. Mark is content to affirm that God will bring Jesus among them again, but he does not depict that event. The faithful reader of Mark is persuaded as to what did happen. The nonbeliever who reads Mark is challenged to investigate how that claim fared in the light of subsequent events. Paul enumerates the appearances of the risen Jesus to Peter, to other disciples, to hundreds of others, and finally to himself (1 Cor 15:3–8), as we noted earlier. That event is as real to him and to the other witnesses who claim to have seen him risen from the dead as are the events reported in the rest of the gospel tradition. Mark is content to conclude his gospel with an open-ended account. The other Gospels, as we shall note in the next chapter, provide what their writers considered to be specific and concrete evidence for their claims that Jesus rose from the dead.

Although Mark did not write his gospel according to the conventions of modern history writing, it is important to observe that the issues that are central in his narrative are precisely those that we have seen to be present in the non-New Testament writings of the early Roman period where Jesus is mentioned. These issues are (1) his death by crucifixion under order from Pontius Pilate; (2) the claim that he performed extraordinary deeds, and that he did so without the approval of the established authorities; (3) his obscure origins in a small provincial town; and (4) that the movement he launched survived his death. What Mark provides is a series of detailed traditions that clarify each of these issues and that offer the reader an explanation – from the point of view of a group of his followers more than three decades after his death – of what lay behind these widely perceived historical traditions about Jesus.

There can be no doubt that Mark's account is written from the perspective of a group of those who believe that Jesus is indeed God's agent for the establishment of his New Covenant people and for the renewal of the creation. Mark is not an objective historian, but every historian is consciously or unconsciously writing from a point of view and with a set of implicit values and assumptions. Mark makes many of his convictions explicit. We have noted that at many points the private explanations that are offered, as well as the stylized interpretation of some of the sayings of Jesus, seem to reflect the needs and circumstances of the church a generation after the time of Jesus. But that does not require that we dismiss these traditions as of no historical value. Through both the older and the later tradition in Mark and in Q, there is a consistent picture of Jesus that matches well with what we learn about him from extrabiblical sources. We shall see in the following chapter how this mix of old and later tradition is apparent in Matthew, Luke, and John, as it is in Q and Mark. But we shall also see how freely the tradition is expanded and fundamentally altered in the interests of issues and problems that arose in the church of the late first and the second century.

Chapter 5

What Can We Learn from the Other Gospels?

In our analysis of Q and Mark, there have been references to the evidence that Matthew, Luke, and John have developed in their respective ways the Markan practice of adapting the Jesus tradition to the altered circumstances and needs of their own communities in the later years of the first century. In some cases, these later writers may have included important early historical material, and we shall note that possibility as we examine each of the Gospels. But we shall also sketch the special aims and needs in the light of which each writer has shaped the gospel material. That these other Gospels are given a briefer treatment is a reflection of two factors: (1) the later date of their writing, which removes them farther in time and circumstance from the events they report; and (2) the fact that much of the historical material they do include (often with significant modification) is derived from Q and Mark, two of the sources that we have already examined in some detail. To pose the basic question of this book in altered form, what does each of these other Gospels contribute to our knowledge of Jesus, and of the process of appropriation and use of that tradition in the early Christian communities?

Luke's Literary Skills

Luke stands out from the other three Gospels in a way that is of importance for our investigation: He presents his story of Jesus and the early church in a literary style that reflects the approach of historians of his time. It is clear that he wants the thoughtful

89

reader of the late first or early second century to read his account of Jesus and the apostles in a form compatible with the literary features that they would have been accustomed to in other historical writings. The links with contemporary historical style are evident in some superficial ways, such as Luke's mention of others who have written on the same subject, his claim to be writing "an orderly account," and his mention of his patron, Theophilus, under whose auspices he is writing his two-volume work (Lk 1:1–4). More important, however, are his claims to have had transmitted to him information from eyewitnesses, and to have "followed all things closely." Still more significant – indeed, unique among the Gospels' writers – is Luke's having moved beyond the story of Jesus to offer his account in Acts of the spread of Christianity from the origins in Jerusalem to the symbolic center of the pagan world, Rome.

One must keep in mind, however, that historians in this period were not interested simply in reporting events of the past, but saw their role as providing the meaning of those past events for readers in the present. This approach is, of course, typical of historians throughout the ages, but in the time of Luke they did not adopt the pose of objectivity, as though they were merely telling "how it really happened." That posture developed in the late eighteenth and early nineteenth centuries, and is still represented in the self-delusions of some modern historians. In the ancient world there was more candor on this subject: The historians were not detached reporters, but sought to reconstruct the events of the past in light of some larger significance for the readers in the present. Luke makes this clear: He wants his readers "to know the truth concerning the things about which [they] have been informed" (Lk 1:4).

Having acknowledged that Luke has a case to present by means of his historical account, we should not dismiss his work as of no historical value. Indeed, we can check his use of sources by comparing Mark and Q with what he makes of them. The results are to show that he depends heavily on both of them, and that he almost certainly reproduced the Q material more faithfully than Matthew does, including even the original order of Q. Some scholars think that he even follows more closely than Matthew the original order of the Q source. In any case, our reconstruction of Q has been largely dependent on Luke, who reproduces more primitive forms of the sayings of Jesus, whereas Matthew has adapted them more freely to his own purposes. We can assume, therefore, that Luke is a responsible historian in his use of sources.

Luke and the Inclusive Message of Jesus

What are the characteristic features that come through in Luke's portrait of Jesus? Throughout his gospel, Luke wants to show the continuities and the transforming differences between what was announced and expected in the Old Testament and what happened in the coming of Jesus. This feature is by no means unique to Luke, but is found in the other Gospels – indeed, in all the other New Testament writings – and very likely in the teachings of Jesus himself. As we noted in our examination of Q, in answer to the question from John the Baptist about what Jesus expected to do and who he was, Jesus responded in language that is a mosaic of quotes from the prophets of Israel. All these point to his seeing himself as the channel of God's grace to the deprived, the needy, and those excluded on ritual grounds from participation in God's people (Lk 7:22). What is important for Jesus and for Luke is that these attitudes and activities of Jesus are in conformity with the Scriptures.

Luke develops this theme from the outset in his account of the circumstances surrounding the birth of Jesus. The birth of John the Baptist is described in such a way as to point up the parallel between the divine grace that gave a son, Samuel, to an aged couple and the coming of John (1 Sm 1–3; Lk 1:5–25, 57–80). Just as Samuel's climactic act was to anoint David as king (1 Sm 16), so the peak of John's career as Luke reports it comes in his baptism of Jesus and the gift of the Spirit (Lk 3:21–2). Jesus' birth was prepared for by the outpouring of the Spirit (Lk 1:34) in fulfillment of prophetic hopes, as Jesus reportedly makes explicit in Luke 4:16–21. Even Luke's version of the genealogy of Jesus (Lk 3:23–8) traces his origins back to Adam, whom Israel saw as the founder of the human race, rather than to Abraham, the father of the Jewish people, as Matthew's genealogy does (Mt 1:2). And Mary's song at the prospect of Jesus' birth announces the coming change when the poor, the hungry, and the powerless will be exalted by God (Lk 1:46–55). Similarly, Simeon's blessing of the infant Jesus predicts that through this child, God has prepared a "light for the Gentiles," as well as glory for Israel (Lk 2:31–2).

The links with the hopes of Israel are explicit in these stories of Jesus' birth and childhood. His birthplace is Bethlehem, famed as the city of David, and hence the symbolic location for his prophesied successor, the Messiah, to begin his work (Lk 2:1–4). The Holy Family returns to Jerusalem, in keeping with the pattern of Jewish piety, for the circumcision of Jesus (2:21–40) and at the Passover (2:41–52). It is while there on this festal occasion that Jesus becomes separated from his family, because he "must be occupied with his Father's affairs" (2:49).

The stage for Jesus' activity in Luke's narrative is set by John the Baptist, who declares that ethnic membership in God's people is no guarantee for being right with God (3:7–9) and that tax collectors and even pagan soldiers who are penitent have a right to participation in God's new people (3:7–14). When John's appearance on the scene is first announced by Luke, the Scriptures quoted to explain what he is doing reach their climax in the promise, "And all humanity shall see the salvation of God" (3:2–6). Here, as throughout Luke and Acts, the reader is reminded that these events took place in the context of pagan history and during the reign of pagan rulers (Lk 1:5; 2:1; 3:1; 23:6–7).

Jesus' understanding of the task to which God called him, as Luke portrays it, is given in detail through the quotation from Isaiah 61 in Luke 4:18–19, which announces that he is to preach good news to the poor, to proclaim release and liberty to those who are bound, and recovery of sight to the blind. This is followed by Jesus' bold claim that we noted earlier: "This scripture has now been fulfilled among you." He is reported as going on to justify this outreach and this liberation activity by appeal to the examples of Elijah and Elisha, the Old Testament prophets whose works in the name of the God of Israel extended to non-Israelites, like the Sidonian woman (1 Kgs 17:8–9) and the leper from Syria (2 Kgs 5:14). In the Q tradition that Luke incorporates here, that program is confirmed in Jesus' response to the questions addressed by John the Baptist from prison, in which Jesus' special concern is for those regarded by the Jews as excluded from participation in God's people: the blind, the lame, lepers, the deaf, the dead (Lk 7:22). Unique to Luke is the story of the ten lepers whom Jesus healed (17:11–19). Those who hear in faith his message are these marginal, deprived persons, shut off from access to God by ethnic and ritual boundaries of Jewish piety in this period, as we noted in our review of the Q tradition in Chapter 3.

Luke reinforces this impression of Jesus as including outsiders in his mission through his use of material from Q and from his own unique sources. The healing of the son of the Roman officer (7:1–10) makes this point, as do the accounts of his restoring to life the son of a widow from the city of Nain (where Jesus lost his ritual purity by touching the bier of the dead young man, 7:11–17), and his acceptance of the anointing by the "sinful woman" (7:36–50). Indeed, the important roles of women in the stories Luke reports are relatively rare in either pagan or Jewish literature of this period.[1] For example, Luke alone mentions the women who form a financial support group for Jesus and his followers (8:1–3) and his association with Mary and Martha (10:38–42). These pictures of the inclusion of women in the movement are expanded by the stories of their important witness at the Crucifixion (23:27–31) and at the empty tomb. Luke's report is expanded from Mark (Lk 24:1–11) and then is richly extended in Acts by the narratives of various roles for women in the early Christian communities.

Luke's portrayal of Jesus as especially concerned for the poor is matched in this gospel by his denunciation of the rich. The poor and the hungry, whose blessedness is pronounced by Jesus (6:20–49), are seen as literally and not merely spiritually deprived, as in Matthew 5:3–6. But in addition, Luke adds woes to the rich and comfortable (Lk 6:24–6). Later come warnings to the rich fool, who is complacent in his affluence (12:13–21) and the familiar contrast between the rich man and the impoverished Lazarus (16:19–31).

Other Lukan stories that stress the inclusiveness of Jesus are the report of his compassion toward the Samaritans (9:51–6) and the vivid account of the Samaritan who is so generous toward one who is in need (10:29–37); the story of the repentant tax collector (18:9–14); and Jesus' welcome to Zaccheus and subsequent fellowship with this tax collector in Jericho (19:1–10). Luke supplements the Markan account of Jesus' sending out the twelve on a mission of healing and preaching (which in Matthew is limited to Israel; Mt 10:6) with a story of his sending out seventy missioners and welcoming them on their return (Lk 10:1–20). What is significant is that for Jews of this period, seventy was the number of the nations of the world, so that Jesus' second sending of his followers anticipates

1. For example, in a second-century B.C. decree of the Roman Senate, the cult of Bacchus (the god of wine), which was reportedly promoted by women, was denounced as scandalous and outlawed.

the mission to all nations that Luke describes in Acts 1–2, as authorized by the outpouring of the Holy Spirit at Pentecost.

Equally important for Luke is his portrayal of God as concerned to seek out and accept those outsiders. This is clear in the three uniquely Lukan parables of Luke 15 that depict God in three images: (1) the shepherd who rejoices at the recovery of a lost sheep; (2) the housewife who rejoices at the recovery of a lost coin; and (3) the climactic portrayal of God in the story of the father rejoicing at the restoration of his estranged son (Lk 15:1–10). Preceding this section is another parable from the Q source, in which (as we noted earlier) the invitation to share in God's coming Kingdom is compared with an invitation to a banquet that is spurned by those originally invited, and that is accepted by the very types of persons whom Luke has presented as the objects of Jesus' and God's special concern: the poor, the maimed, the blind, the lame (14:15–24).

There are also significant omissions or reductions in Luke, as compared with the other Gospels. The controversies of Jesus with the Pharisees, which figure so importantly in Matthew, and the predictions about the coming destruction of the Temple and the end of the present age are played down somewhat by Luke, because one of his major interests is to show that the people of God include both Jews and Gentiles. He has his own version of the Last Supper, in which the emphasis falls on the nature of the New Covenant people that Jesus is establishing (22:15–20; 22:27–30). And the stories of the appearances of Jesus after the Resurrection go beyond what is merely promised in Mark, and seem clearly to reflect the practices of the early church, including the Christians' study and interpretation of the Old Testament and the celebration of the Lord's Supper (24:32, 35). Luke alone describes Jesus as interpreting in all the Scriptures (the Law, the prophets, and the other writings) the "things concerning himself" and as being "made known [to the gathered community] in the breaking of bread." Other distinctive features of Luke include the "promise of my Father" (that the Spirit will be poured out on his people) and the account of the Ascension referred to briefly in Luke (24:49–53), which describe events that he will report in greater detail in the opening chapters of Acts.

On our central question of historical knowledge of Jesus, it is impossible to determine with certainty how much of Luke's special material goes back to Jesus, but his major emphases – Jesus' concern for and invitation to the marginal people of his day – certainly match well with the themes that come through in our oldest sources. As would be the case with any historian writing in any epoch, Luke's story reflects the interests and concerns of his own situation. But it also seems to reflect faithfully the major characteristic of Jesus' public activity, which was in turn the major reason for the opposition he evoked from the religious leaders of his time: the redefining of Covenant relationship with God on an inclusive basis.

Matthew: Jesus as the Founder of the True Israel

Matthew was written in the latter part of the first century at the time when the Pharisees, with the apparent encouragement of the Roman authorities in Palestine, were at work formulating the basic guidelines that were to give shape to rabbinic Judaism. The Temple and its leadership were gone, as were both the Jewish nationalists (at least, temporarily) and sectarian groups like the Essenes. The major concern of these Jewish leaders was to define the authoritative list of Jewish Scripture, to set up the framework for interpreting it and demonstrating its relevance for their time, and to draw the ritual lines that would mark off their adherents as the true Covenant people. One of the groups they had to differentiate themselves from was the early church. Among the material from this period that seems to have been influenced by the historical developments in this period (see Chapter 4, The Mounting Hostility toward Jesus) was the denunciation of Jesus and his followers. The Christians reacted in a regrettable, though fully human fashion, as Matthew vividly displays in his reconstruction of the story of Jesus.

The pervasive atmosphere of conflict and even the literary arrangement of the material in Matthew reflect this hostile, competitive set of circumstances in which Jesus is depicted as defining the New Covenant community over against that of the Jews. If we assume that the birth stories are Matthew's own introduction to his gospel (Mt 1–2) and that his version of the stories of the Crucifixion, burial, and Resurrection are his conclusion (Mt 26–8), then it appears that Matthew designed his gospel in such a way as to divide his account of Jesus' words and deeds into five sections. Each of these major sections contains a substantial group of sayings, and each ends with some variant of the phrase, "When Jesus had finished . . ." (Mt 7:28–9; 11:1; 13:53; 19:1; 26:1). The first section includes the Sermon on the Mount; the second reports Jesus' instructions to the disciples as they set out on their mission; the third presents Matthew's expanded version of the parables of Jesus; the fourth reports the instructions to the disciples about settling disputes within the community; the fifth presents Matthew's considerably extended version of Jesus' predictions about the coming of the end of the age. It seems that Matthew has developed an intentional parallel to the five books of Moses. That impression is confirmed by the fact that the first of these addresses – the so-called Sermon on the Mount – pictures Jesus on a mountain (like Moses on Sinai), giving his version of instructions to the Covenant people, and in that setting offering repeated contrasts between his understanding of God's will and that of Moses (Mt 5:17–48): "You have heard it was said . . . , but I say to you."

If this proposal about the literary structure of Matthew is

correct, it confirms the theory offered by Krister Stendahl[2] that this book was intended to serve as an orientation for the members of Matthew's community, presenting both the origins of the movement and the regulations for its present members. It would appear, however, that in the intensity of the debate with the Pharisees, the extended discourse section that we know as Matthew 23 was inserted into the document, spoiling the symmetry of the five-part book, but at the same time heightening the tensions with Judaism.

That Matthew was written as a book of orientation and regulations for members of the Matthean community seems clear in that Matthew has converted the promises of Jesus (from the Q source) to the poor and the hungry concerning God's future supply of their needs (Lk 6:20–1) into timeless general statements about the present religious condition of his readers: "Blessed are the poor *in spirit* . . . . Blessed are those who hunger and thirst *for righteousness*" (Mt 5:3–6). Only in Matthew are there expressed the claims that Jesus is the fulfillment of the Law and the prophets, that not the smallest letter of the Law will pass away until everything stated there has been carried out, and that not even the least of the Commandments is to be relaxed by those who seek to enter the Kingdom. The standards of righteousness among the disciples must be higher than those of the scribes and Pharisees if the former are to enter the Kingdom. What seems to have happened is that, under the circumstances in which Matthew is writing, the Christian community has engaged in defining itself over against emergent rabbinic Judaism. Both groups are making competing claims as to which has the proper, divinely determined procedure for interpreting the Law in their present situation.

Throughout his gospel, Matthew stresses the continuity between what God announced through the Law and the prophets

2. In his *School of St. Matthew* (Philadelphia: Fortress, 1968).

and what he is now doing through Jesus. We have already noted that Matthew's genealogy of Jesus focuses on Abraham, the founder of the Covenant people, and David, the ideal king and prototype of the Messiah. The details of his birth are described as in fulfillment of Scripture – both his being born of a virgin (Mt 1:22–3; cf. Is 7:14) and the place of his birth, Bethlehem (Mt 2:4–6; cf. Mi 5:2). The flight of the Holy Family to Egypt and their return are seen as corresponding to the experience of Israel's sojourn in, and return from, Egypt (Mt 2:15; cf. Hos 11:8). Herod's slaughter of the children is seen as a fulfillment of Jeremiah (Mt 2:18; cf. Jer 31:15). The fact is that the exact words of these Scriptures do not fit the situation Matthew is describing. For example, the Hebrew used in Isaiah 7:14 describes a young woman, not necessarily a virgin (although the Greek version uses the term for virgin, *parthenos*), who will conceive and bear a son. But as one can see in the Dead Sea documents, as well as in the prophets and in the Gospels we have already examined, there was no concern for precise correspondence between text and what was seen to be its current meaning. This is particularly clear in Matthew 2:23, which refers to a place-name, Nazareth, that is never mentioned in the Old Testament. But the consonants of this word correspond to the Hebrew *netzer*, which means "sprout" or "shoot," and which is used in Isaiah 11:1 to describe the descendant of David who will accomplish the renewal of God's people.

Many details of Jesus' career are claimed by Matthew to be in fulfillment of Scripture, such as the mixture of Jewish and gentile places where he carried out his preaching ministry (4:15–16; cf. Is 9:1–2), and the rejection of his message (13:14–15; cf. Is 6:9–10). Matthew alters slightly the details of Jesus' entry into Jerusalem, by mentioning two animals for Jesus to ride – apparently because the poetical form of the biblical text of Zechariah 9 refers to two (21:1–9; cf. Zec 9:9). Even the circumstances of the death of the traitor, Judas, are seen to be in accord with Scripture (27:3–10), although the quotation combines elements of Jeremiah 32:6–15 and 18:2–3. It seems plausible that these claims of fulfillment of Scripture are the outcome of later Christian reading of the Old Testament in the light of the events that were remembered in the life and death of Jesus.

Of major importance for Matthew is the fulfillment of "all righteousness" – a phrase that is used as a warrant for John to baptize Jesus (3:15). In the Sermon on the Mount it becomes clear that Christians are to go beyond their Pharisaic contemporaries in fulfilling their obligations to God and their fellow creatures. All three of the key features of rabbinic piety – alms, prayer, and fasting – are set forth by Jesus as obligatory for his followers (6:1–18). Although Matthew reproduces Jesus' explanation as to why his disciples do not fast (Mk 2:18–20; cf. Mt 9:14–15), in 6:16–18 fasting is actually commended, so long as it is not a form of religious showing off. The instructions about prayer reproduce the Q tradition of the so-called Lord's Prayer (Lk 11:2–4), but set it out in an elaborated liturgical style (6:9–13). In contrast to Mark's report of Jesus' complete rejection of the practice of divorce and remarriage (10:11–12), however, Matthew twice allows for it, if the partner has been unfaithful (Mt 5:31–2; 10:9). This suggests that Matthew's community has relaxed the strictness of what was likely Jesus' attitude on the subject. Although the unique passage in Matthew about eunuchs is puzzling (19:10–12), it seems to imply that Jesus encouraged at least some of his followers to abstain from sexual relationships. In this connection, it is worth noting that Paul describes the apostles as being accompanied in their travels by their wives (1 Cor 9:5), which makes it evident that in spite of this saying in Matthew, celibacy was not the rule among the first generation of Christians.

Throughout Matthew there is evidence of basic shifts in the way in which covenantal participation is defined. Initially, the focus of the mission of Jesus and his followers is depicted as the people of historic Israel. When he sends out the twelve, he tells them to limit their activities to "the lost sheep of the house of Israel" (10:6). Yet the parables in the latter chapters of Matthew – some of which are found only here and others that are significantly modified from the more original versions in Mark or Q – point to the claim that after Israel has had its opportunity to hear the message and has rejected it, it will go out to those considered outsiders by the norms of Jewish piety. The Parable of the Laborers in the Vineyard (20:1–16) expresses the resentment of those who were earlier called by God against those who came much later – that is, Gentiles and the unclean. The same point is made in the Parable of the Two Sons (21:28–32), where it is asserted that tax collectors and harlots will enter the kingdom before the pious do, because the former repented and the latter did not. In the Parable of the Vineyard Workers (21:33–46), the same basic point as in the Markan version is made: that the workers in God's vineyard have rejected his messengers, culminating in their rejection of Jesus. But Matthew adds that the owner of the vineyard "will put to death those miserable wretches" and give the vineyard to others. It is explicitly stated that the Kingdom of God will be taken away from the Jewish leaders "and given to a nation producing the fruits of it." Lest any reader miss the point, Matthew adds that the leaders "perceived that he was speaking about them" (21:45).

Similarly, in the Parable of the Marriage Feast (22:1–14), Matthew has modified the Q tradition in several significant ways: The host is now a king; the banquet is a wedding feast, which was a Jewish symbol for the consummation of God's purpose for his people; the rejection of the invitation leads to the sending of troops and the destruction of their city (an obvious reference to the Roman destruction of Jerusalem); and the wedding guest without the proper garment seems to be one

who enters the Kingdom without the proper cloak of righteousness.

Israel's lack of preparation for the coming of God's agent to
call human beings to account is conveyed in two parables: the
ten maidens (25:1–13) and that of the talents (25:14–30), where
there is accountability for the responsibilities that have been
placed on the servants of the owner. Implied in these is a delay
in God's calling his people to account – on the Day of Judgment – and as a result, an anticipation of mixed responses and
failed responsibilities on the part of those who claim to be
God's people. The importance of enduring and of maintaining
one's righteousness is dramatically stated in two other parables
unique to Matthew: that of the mixture of weeds and wheat
(13:24–30), and that of the net that gathers good and bad fish
(13:47–50). In the explanations that accompany these parables,
the community is pictured as regrettably combining in its
membership those who are worthy and those who are not – the
righteous and the evil. This implies a situation in which the
church as an ongoing institution has members whose interests
and commitments have waned, or who have abandoned the
faith.

In all four of the Gospels, the only mention of the church by
the term *ekklesia* is in Matthew. In his account of Peter's confession of Jesus' messiahship (which is stated more formally
than in Mark – cf. Mt 16:16 with Mk 8:29), Jesus responds by
telling Peter that God is going to build a church and that the
church will endure in the face of diabolical opposition (16:17–
18). Protestants have tended to assume that the "rock" on
which the church is built is Peter's confession, whereas Roman
Catholics see Peter as the apostolic foundation of the church.
But in either case, Matthew writes that to him and his associates is granted the decision-making power to determine who is
in the community and who should be excluded (16:19). These
decisions receive divine confirmation as well. In 18:15–20 the

procedure is laid down for settling disputes within the church, again with the promise of divine confirmation. There can be no doubt that for Matthew, Jesus has authorized the establishment of an institutional structure, with the right to control membership and to resolve conflicts among the members. It is not a fully developed ecclesiastical hierarchy, but the major responsibility rests with the followers of Jesus in their apostolic role.

Scattered throughout Matthew are passages unique to this gospel that portray a range of roles to be filled within the church. In 23:34 there is mention of others, in addition to the disciples, who represent Jesus in the mission to the wider world: prophets, wise men, and scribes. In the Parable of the Last Judgment (Mt 25:31–46), those who represent Jesus in preparing for the coming of God's Rule include some who are designated simply as "little ones." How their hearers and pupils respond to them determines their fate in the age to come. In 13:51 there is some additional detail about the function in Matthew's community of the "scribe" who has been "trained for the kingdom of God" (13:51). Just in this period of Judaism there rose to leadership those who devoted themselves to the interpretation of the Law and who were accordingly known as "bookmen," from the Hebrew term *sopherim*, which derives from *sepher*, meaning "book" – or "The Book." Christians, Matthew tells us, have the counterpart of these officials in the church. Their task is to give a Christian understanding of the Law and the prophets in light of the teaching of Jesus as it has been preserved in their community.

These competitive enterprises between emergent rabbinic Judaism and the institutional form of the church inevitably fostered hostility. Accordingly, the Christians are warned of persecutions they might expect at the hands of the Jewish leaders (10:17), as well as the prospect of being summoned before the secular authorities (10:18). The hostility of the religious leaders is heightened by Matthew at several points in his account of the trial and execution of Jesus, as when they accept responsibility for the death of Jesus (27:25) and when they bribe the soldiers to report that the disciples had stolen the body of Jesus (28:11–15). The ultimate fate of every member of the human race is said by Matthew to turn on their response to the "little ones" who are Jesus' messengers and agents to call the nations of the world to repentance and to lead them to an understanding of God's purpose (25:31–46). To receive these "little ones" and their message brings an eternal reward; to reject them brings eternal punishment.

Meanwhile, the disciples are reported by Matthew (28:16–20) as having been charged by the risen Jesus to go into all the world, to make disciples of all the nations, to perform the central ritual of baptism according to the Trinitarian formula. All this is to be carried out through the authority that Jesus transmitted to his disciples. It is not surprising that the church in the early centuries should place Matthew at the head of its canon of Scripture, since it most clearly reflects the shift of the Christian movement from its original intensely expectant period of concentrating on getting the message out as widely and as soon as possible (as in Mark and Q) to the later stage in which guidelines must be laid down about internal order and external relationships.

John: Jesus as Agent of the New Symbolic World

John differs from the other Gospels in structure, in strategy, and in detail of his account. This is evident from the opening lines of his prologue (1:1–18). In words that recall the opening of Genesis ("In the beginning . . ."), John pictures the agent of God, the Word, who was the instrument through whom the world was created, and who now has come in human form ("the Word became flesh," 1:14) to live on earth and to invite people to share

in the light of the knowledge of God that he brings (1:9–12).
That Word who is the revelation of God is contrasted by John
with the Law, which was given through Moses. It is Jesus who
discloses God's grace and truth (1:18). John is building on the
Jewish idea of wisdom as God's agent in creating and sustaining
the world. But what is radically new is John's claim that Jesus is
the wisdom and purpose of God in a fully human form. The fact
that John's term for the agent of God is not "sophia" (the ordinary word for wisdom) but "logos," shows that the author wants
also to link Jesus with the Hellenistic concept of a rationale that
is basic to the created order and in the movement of human
history.

As John's account of Jesus' career and teaching begins, we
hear nothing of the circumstances of his birth, other than that
he is the son of Joseph and comes from Nazareth (1:45). Later,
his mother, Mary, is mentioned as being present at the wedding
in Cana, but when she asks him to help the hosts, whose supply of wine is running out, he puts her off with a strange remark, "What is that to me and to you?" (2:1–4). The miracle
that Jesus then performs – the changing of water into wine –
shows that his action in this situation has a great deal of meaning, not only for Jesus and his mother, but also for the whole
community for which John is writing. The multiple meanings
of the Johannine material are apparent when one considers that
marriage is an important Old Testament image of the relationship of God and his people, as the sad account in Hosea 1–3
of Israel's unfaithfulness as the wife of Yahweh shows. The
same notion of Israel as the wayward bride appears throughout
Jeremiah. The Song of Solomon, on the other hand, was in-
terpreted by the Jews as an allegory of the fulfillment of the
relationship between God and his people. It is this joyful significance of marriage that is implied in John 2, where the wedding symbolizes the consummation of God's purpose for his
people. At the same time, the two elements in use at the wed-

ding feast have yet another kind of symbolic meaning and point to the two basic sacraments of the church: the water "for cleansing" in baptism, and the wine of fulfillment in the New Covenant.

Jesus' action is described by John as "the first of his signs" and as the means by which he "manifested his glory" (2:11). At the end of the main part of his gospel (20:30–1), John declares that these signs were done and have been reported by him so that Jesus' disciples and John's readers might believe that Jesus is the Christ, and have life through his name. The miracles, therefore, will not convince outsiders, but will convey to believers who Jesus is and what God is doing through him.

The "signs" that John reports consist of the miracles Jesus does: the healing of the officer's son (4:46–54); the healing of the paralytic at the pool (5:2–14); the feeding of the five thousand and Jesus' walking on the sea (6:1–21); the restoration of sight to the man born blind (9:1–12); and the raising of Lazarus from the dead (11:1–44). Some interpreters of John would include among the signs the stories of his encounters with such persons as the Jewish ruler Nicodemus (3:1–15), the conversation with the woman of Samaria (4:1–42), and the public and private statements of Jesus reported in John 7–8.

The other identifiable group of traditions about Jesus in John are those in which Jesus identifies himself through the use of the phrase "I am." This expression in Greek is the way that the translators of the Hebrew Bible into Greek understood the sacred name of God, Yahweh, as in Exodus 3:14. There Moses is commissioned by God to lead his people out of Egypt and to call them to Covenant relationship with Yahweh. When Moses asks whom he shall say has sent him, God replies, "I Am has sent you." The occurrences of this phrase in John are linked with specific roles of Jesus:

> I am the bread of life (6:35);
> I am the light of the world (8:1);

Before Abraham came into being, I am (8:58);
I am the door (10:7);
I am the good shepherd (10:11);
I am the resurrection and the life (11:25);
I am the way, the truth and the life (14:6);
I am the vine, you are the branches (15:1, 5);
I am [he] (18:5).

This final instance of the "I am" phrase is the more striking, because it is spoken in response to the statement of the soldiers who have come to seize him that they are looking for Jesus of Nazareth. Yet in the trial scenes that follow, the authorities are unable to make Jesus commit himself as to his identity (Jn 18). The reader is expected to know that this Jesus of Nazareth is one with "I am," the God of the Covenant.

This double-meaning response to the soldier's question is characteristic of John's gospel throughout, since he portrays Jesus as frequently speaking on two levels: literally and symbolically. For example, when Jesus tells Nicodemus that the Son of man must be lifted up as Moses lifted up the serpent in the wilderness (3:14–15), the point is not merely that Jesus will be lifted up on the cross as the remedy for human sin, as the serpent was for the sinful Israelites in Numbers 21. He will also be lifted up in the Resurrection, and then draw all who believe in him to share in eternal life.

The "I am" sayings in John's gospel serve much the same end that the reports of Jesus' sayings and actions do in the other Gospels: Jesus is God's medium of communication with his people, and the roles he fulfills are metaphors of the new relationship God is establishing with the Covenant community. As the bread of life, Jesus is the means by which God's people are sustained and able to live. Through Jesus the light of the knowledge of God goes out to the whole world, even though not all respond in faith. God's purpose through Jesus is older and more basic than even the establishment of the Covenant with Abraham. Jesus the door provides access to God for his people; at the same time, he nurtures and protects them as shepherd of the flock of God. He is the embodiment of the renewal of life, the way to reach God, and the truth about him. The living link that Jesus embodies between God and his people enables them to live morally and spiritually productive lives. In short, he is the incarnation of the God whose name is "I Am." In spite of this highly symbolic style of narrating the story of Jesus, John does include what may well be some historical details that are obscured or omitted in the other Gospels. One of these is the implication in John 1 and 3:22–4:1 that Jesus was for a time a follower of John the Baptist, and that he carried on baptizing activity in competition with John. The other bit of information concerns the date of the final meal of Jesus with his disciples. The other Gospels imply that this was a Passover meal. Because the date of this feast was determined by the phases of the moon, it could occur on any day of the week. John states, however, that Jesus' last meal was on the night before the Passover, which would then have begun at sundown on Friday, as the Sabbath began. The historical and symbolic meaning would converge, according to John: As the Passover lambs were being killed in preparation for Israel's celebration of the historic feast, Jesus, the Lamb of God (1:29), was being put to death outside the city "for the sins of the world."

While any historical account is a blend of reporting what happened and interpreting its significance, John clearly lets the weight fall on the latter factor. In several places, he does not bother to finish the narrative once his basic points have been made. This is the case in the account of Jesus' interchange with Nicodemus. In other passages, the report of what Jesus did and said slides over into an elaborate explanation of meaning, as in the contrast between the Old Covenant people, Israel, and the new people that Jesus is calling into being (Jn 6). Similarly, the interchange with his critics in John 8 becomes an elaborate statement of the difference between Abraham as founder of the

Old Covenant people and Jesus as the one who is convening the New Covenant community.

These symbolic descriptions of the new people of God anticipate the inclusion of the gentiles: Greeks, as John calls them (Jn 12:20) or "other sheep which are not of this fold" (10:16). What Jesus does is in contrast with the traditional feasts in which Israel celebrated its origins and its preservation by God: Passover (deliverance from Egyptian bondage, 12:1), Tabernacles (God's leading of his people through the desert to the land of promise, 7:2), and Dedication (the rededication of the Temple in the days of the Maccabees, when national autonomy was regained, 10:22). Jesus' role in each case is seen to transcend the historic experience of Israel under its leaders, and to lead to the establishment of the New Covenant people, which know no ethnic, ritual, or historical prerequisites for admission.

The new community is depicted as organic in nature, with such images as the flock of God (Jn 10) or the vine and branches (Jn 15). Both these images appear in the Old Testament, but the emphasis in John falls on the life shared in common by the leader and the people. The instrument of that life is the Spirit, which God will pour out on his people when Jesus has been taken up to God. The Spirit will be the agent of divine instruction and enablement in the new community. That group, according to John 13, is to be seen as having little by way of leadership or authority structure. Its members are bound together by love and mutual concern, even to the extent of laying down their lives for others. The nearest approach to Matthew's view of the disciples as decision makers within the community is in the granting or withholding of the forgiveness of sins. Indeed, the members are not differentiated in terms of role or authority, but are called simply to love one another (13:34). In the epilogue (Jn 21), they are told to feed the other members of the flock, which seems to mean to instruct them. The only qualification for membership in this community is to see in

Jesus the light of the knowledge of God, the one whose death and resurrection are the manifestations of God's love for the world (1:12; 3:16).

These three Gospels serve two important functions in our quest for knowledge about Jesus. First, they confirm the basic pattern that we saw to be present in the oldest traditions about Jesus, and in the other New Testament writings: Jesus as the one who calls together the new people of God, who manifests the power of God overcoming evil and human sin, and whose death is seen as the seal of the New Covenant relationship. Second, the range of differences in content and emphases among these writings reminds us that each of the Gospels was written in a different set of circumstances, with different concerns and aims represented by its author. What we see in the Gospels is not only the passing on of the traditions about Jesus, but evidence of the adaptation of that tradition in order to address more appropriately the needs of the young churches in varying cultural and religious circumstances.

Conclusion

What does this survey of the evidence tell us that we can know about Jesus? A great deal!

First, we see that the issues with which he was dealing and that led to his rejection by the religious authorities were precisely those questions and concerns that were central for the various Jewish groups that were contemporary with him. Chief among these were three questions: (1) What are the qualifications for membership in God's Covenant people? (2) How does one maintain status within that people? (3) Who is the agent of God through whom this renewal will take place? Instead of the ritual and ethnic requirements considered essential by groups that differed among themselves – the priests and Sadducees, the Essenes and the Pharisees – Jesus invited into the fellowship of his followers all who were willing to acknowledge their need of God's grace and to see Jesus as God's instrument for the renewal of the Covenant. Thus, from the beginning of his activity, those who were ruled to be outsiders by the religious standards of his Jewish contemporaries he declared to be forgiven, healed, and accepted by God.

This role clearly implied that he saw himself in a special relation to God. To describe this relation he and his followers used such terms as Messiah, Son of God, and Son of Man; yet they did so in ways that were based not on his fulfillment of but his transformation of the royal and priestly functions in keeping with the history and the expectations of Israel. The supreme irony is that he was executed by the Romans on the ground of a claim he himself rejected: that in the political sense, he was the king of Israel. He predicted the destruction of the Temple and the end of its ritual system, and offered no prophecy that it or its priesthood had any further role in the purpose of God for his people. God was to be present in the midst of his people as they met in table fellowship, not as they gathered in a grand sacred building. By the time our Gospels are written, however, the process of adaptation of the earliest Jesus tradition to the changing circumstances of the new community is apparent. Thus the formalization of what began in the Jesus movement as a simple meal into a clerically administered sacrament is analogous to the shift from the informal gatherings of Jesus' followers to the ecclesiastical patterns and structures evident in the later books of the New Testament. This is especially evident, for example, in the Letter to the Hebrews, where Jesus is portrayed in the role of the great high priest who enters with his own sacrifices into the presence of God (Heb 9:11–28).

At the root of these later developments, however, were Jesus' convictions about himself and the new people God was calling him to gather. In the Gospels, the basis for ratification of the New Covenant was his own death, which was recalled symbolically in the broken loaf and the shared wine. And beyond his own impending death, Jesus foresaw that God would act to vindicate him and his faithful followers and that they would one day be reunited in fellowship in a new age.

His healings and exorcisms were offered as evidence that through him God was preparing the created order for the coming of God's Rule in its fullness. His willingness to touch persons afflicted by diseases that rendered them unclean by prevailing Jewish standards and to welcome them into the fellowship of his followers is further evidence of his radical revision of God's attitude toward those who, by legal tradition, were outsiders to the religious community.

His picture of God was of one who was actively concerned to

bring into relation with himself those who on moral or ritual grounds would have been excluded. His interpretation of the Law stressed the ways in which love and concern could be shown to others, rather than the standards that were required if one were to maintain good standing within the holy people. Love of neighbor, which is taught in the Jewish Bible (Lv 19:18), is extended by Jesus to mean that one's neighbor is not merely another Jew with whom one comes in contact, but any person of any ethnic origin whom one finds to be in need. Purity of heart, or integrity of motive, is essential for God's people, not ritual purity. Akin to this is Jesus' unqualified commitment to the will of God, even to the point of accepting one's own death. On this, of course, he was not merely instructor but also chief example.

There comes from Jesus the conviction that death is not the end or the defeat of God's purpose, however, but that through and beyond death God will be at work achieving his purpose for his people. The circle of Jesus' followers was persuaded that God had demonstrated the validity of this expectation by raising Jesus from the dead.

The Jesus tradition was received and transmitted in a variety of forms by those who lived and wrote in a variety of contexts over the decades that followed the death of Jesus. It need not surprise or disquiet us that the story of Jesus and the reports of his teachings have come down to us in significantly different accounts. The two oldest forms in which the tradition has been preserved – Q and Mark – confirm one another in historically important ways. Some of this gospel material receives additional confirmation from traces of the Jesus tradition in the letters of Paul. Through the Gospels we may see how, in detail, the circumstances and life situation of those who wrote down the records of Jesus inform us about them and their respective communities, just as they provide us with knowledge about Jesus. Many of the details of these accounts of Jesus receive confirmation and even clarification from sources outside the Gospels, including non-Christian sources. In spite of this range of ways in which the tradition about Jesus has been transmitted, we have available a clear and remarkably consistent array of evidence about this figure whose life, teachings, and death have continued to have such a profound and enduring impact on the subsequent history of the human race.

Questions for Exploration

1. What kinds of sources are available for providing knowledge about Jesus? What are some of the major points about him on which the sources converge?
2. What is our oldest source for the early Christian tradition about Jesus' words and deeds, and what kinds of information does it provide?
3. In what ways does this evidence show the contrasts between Jesus' defining the people of God and the definitions offered by his Jewish contemporaries?
4. By the Jewish standards of the first century, what was required for Gentiles to approach the God of Israel? What did Jesus require for them to come to God?
5. What aspects of Jesus' career are described by Mark in our earliest gospel? What is Jesus' role in the purpose of God according to Mark?
6. Why do Mark and Paul place so much emphasis on the death and resurrection of Jesus?
7. Why was Jesus' announcement of the destruction of the Temple such an important issue for his Jewish contemporaries? What did it mean for Mark and the early Christians?
8. In what ways do Matthew and Luke develop the claims of the early Christians that Jesus is the fulfillment of the Jewish Scriptures?
9. How does Matthew sharpen the contrast between Jewish understanding of the obligation to keep the Law of Moses and Jesus' standards for life in the new community?

115

10. How does Luke develop the emphasis on the teaching of Jesus on the inclusion of Gentiles, tax collectors, and sinners in the new people of God?
11. What are some of the ways in which the Gospel of John retells the story of Jesus in order to communicate the significance of Jesus to Jews and Gentiles seeking direct, personal participation in religious experience of God?
12. What are some of the ways in which the gospel tradition was expanded and changed in the Christian writings of the second century?

Suggestions for Further Reading

A more technical analysis of the gospel sources and other historical references to Jesus may be found in my *Jesus in History: An Approach to the Study of the Gospels*, 2nd ed. (New York: Harcourt Brace Jovanovich, 1977). Discussion of the questions of historical reliability are offered by A. E. Harvey in *Jesus and the Constraints of History* (Philadelphia: Westminster, 1982) and by Gerard S. Sloyan, *Jesus in Focus* (Mystic, Conn.: Twenty-Third Publications, 1983).

A fine commentary on Mark is Dennis E. Nineham, *Saint Mark*, Pelican Commentary Series (Baltimore and Hammondsworth: Penguin, 1963). My own study of Mark is *Community of the New Age* (1977; reprint, Macon, Ga.: Mercer University Press, 1983). A fine set of essays on Matthew prepared and introduced by Graham Stanton is *The Interpretation of Matthew* (London: SPCK, and Philadelphia: Fortress, 1983). An excellent commentary on Luke is that of Eduard Schweizer, *The Good News According to Luke* (London: SPCK, and Atlanta: John Knox, 1984).

Studies of the Gospel of John include L. Louis Martyn, *History and Theology in the Fourth Gospel* (New York: Harper & Row, 1968), and Raymond E. Brown, *The Community of the Beloved Disciple* (New York: Paulist Press, 1979).

Index

SCRIPTURAL REFERENCES

Old Testament

Old Testament Pseudepigrapha

Apocryphal New Testament

Greek Papyri